His Holiness the Dalai Lama

Teachings in Los Angeles, California
June, 1997

June 5-7

Commentary on
The *Precious Garland* of Ācārya Nāgārjuna

June 8

Empowerment for
the Meditational Practice of Śākyamuni Buddha

PAULEY PAVILION, UCLA

Sponsored by Thubten Dhargye Ling
Venerable Geshe Tsultim Gyeltsen, Director

Note to the Reader

This book has been produced for the special occasion of His Holiness the XIVth Dalai Lama's teachings in Los Angeles in June, 1997. Like the teachings themselves, this book has been sponsored by Thubten Dhargye Ling and its venerable director, Geshe Tsultim Gyeltsen. The book consists primarily of a new translation of the *Precious Garland* of Nāgārjuna, which was undertaken by the translators especially for this auspicious occasion. It is this text which will form the basis of His Holiness's teachings each day on June 5th, 6th, and 7th.

Also included in the Appendix to this volume is an English translation of a special praise to Nāgārjuna, called the *Light of Centrism*, which His Holiness will recite in Tibetan at the beginning of each day of the teachings on the *Precious Garland*. After the recitation of the praise to Nāgārjuna, His Holiness will recite twenty verses from the *Precious Garland* itself (Chapter 5, vv. 66-85). For those who read Tibetan, both the *Light of Centrism* and the verses from the *Precious Garland* have been included in the Appendix in Tibetan script. Brief remarks on the Śākyamuni Empowerment can be found on page 129.

This book was published by Wisdom Publications especially for the occasion of these teachings. This new translation of *Precious Garland* along with His Holiness' comments on the text will be presented in a forthcoming book to be published by Wisdom Publications.

The Precious Garland

An Epistle to a King

Ācārya Nāgārjuna

Translated by

John Dunne & Sara McClintock

Wisdom Publications • Boston

WISDOM PUBLICATIONS
361 NEWBURY STREET
BOSTON, MASSACHUSETTS 02115

"About His Holiness the Dalai Lama" was adapted from *On Common Ground: World Religions in America*, an interactive CD-ROM forthcoming from Columbia University Press. With thanks to Diana Eck and the Pluralism Project, Harvard University.

ISBN 0-86171-132-7

02 01 00 99 98
6 5 4 3 2

Line art: Andy Weber at Manjusri Institute

Designed by: Adie Russell

Wisdom Publications' books are printed on acid-free paper and meet the guidelines for permanence and durability of the Committee on Production Guidelines for Book Longevity of the Council on Library Resources.

Printed in the United States of America

Table of Contents

Translators' Preface

It is difficult to express the extent of our gratitude to those who have made this translation possible. When the Venerable Geshe Gyeltsen of Thubten Dhargye Ling and Tim McNeill of Wisdom Publications proposed that we undertake a new translation of Nāgārjuna's *Precious Garland* for use at a teaching to be given by His Holiness the Dalai Lama, we were naturally both thrilled and honored. Since then, as we have grown more familiar with this profound text, our appreciation of Nāgārjuna's eloquence and insight have grown accordingly. In this concise work, which the great Master wrote in the form of a letter to a king, we encounter a presentation of Buddhism that integrates both worldly and supreme concerns. Here, we discover that Buddhism can be practiced by anyone, even a person involved in the politics of governance. The clear and sagacious advice laid out on every page serves as a road map to one's highest goal—whether that goal concerns more mundane aspirations or the quest for spiritual freedom itself. It is thus with great pleasure and sincere wishes for the benefit of all that we offer this translation to His Holiness the Fourteenth Dalai Lama of Tibet and all of the people who will attend his teachings on this remarkable text.

Nāgārjuna was an Indian Buddhist philosopher, probably of the second century (C.E.), who was renowned for his astute articulation of the Centrist, or Madhyamaka, philosophical view. His presentation of this view, which consists of a thorough-going critique of all forms of essentialism, became a touchstone for the entire Centrist tradition in India and Tibet. His importance for the development not only of the Centrist tradition but of Mahāyāna Buddhism in general can scarcely be exaggerated. His existence traditionally is said to have been predicted by the Buddha Śākyamuni in the 5th century B.C.E., and he has not infrequently been hailed as a "second Buddha" himself. His voluminous writings are codified by the Tibetans in two main groupings: the "corpus on reasoning" (*rigs tshogs*) and the "corpus of praises" (*bstod tshogs*).

The *Precious Garland* falls into the first of these categories, the "corpus on reasoning." The full Sanskrit title of the work is given by the Tibetan translators as the *Rājaparikathāratnamālā*, which can be translated as the *Precious Garland: An Epistle for a King.* An alternative title, recorded in the Tibetan translation of Ajitamitra's Sanskrit commentary, is the *Ratnāvalī*, which conveys essentially the same meaning of a *Precious Garland* or a *Garland of Jewels.* The text is classified by the Tibetan tradition as belonging to the "Epistles" (*sprin yig*) section of the Buddhist canon.

A few words concerning our method of translation and the sources that we used are in order. We prepared our translation by consulting sources in both Sanskrit and Tibetan. For the Sanskrit, the text of which is incomplete, we relied primarily on the edition by Michael Hahn (*Nāgārjuna's Ratnāvalī*, Bonn: Indica et Tibetica Verlag, 1982). We also made reference to the Sanskrit verses as collected by Guiseppe Tucci (*Journal of the Royal Asiatic Society* 1935: 307-25; 1936: 237-52 and 423-35). For the Tibetan, we were fortunately able to consult the excellent critical edition compiled by Ngawang Samten (*Ratnāvalī of Ācārya Nāgārjuna with the commentary by Ajitamitra*, Sarnath: Central Institute of Higher Tibetan Studies, 1990). Since this edition painstakingly records all the variant readings from the various Tibetan canonical collections as well as the Sanskrit manuscripts, it saved us much time and contributed greatly to our ability to translate the text accurately.

To further facilitate our translation, we frequently made use of two excellent commentaries. First, we consulted the *Ratnāvalīṭīkā*, a Sanskrit text attributed to the Indian scholar Ajitamitra (possibly of the eighth century C.E.). This work is preserved in a canonical Tibetan translation and is edited in the above mentioned book by N. Samten. Second, we also relied upon the well known commentary by the Tibetan adept and philosopher Gyaltsab-je (*Rgyal tshab rje Dar ma rin chen*, 1364-1432) called the *Dbu ma rin chen phreng ba'i snying po'i don gsal bar byed pa*, or the *Elucidation of the Essential Meaning of the Madhyamaka Precious Garland*. The edition used comes from volume *ka* in the *Collected Works of Rgyal tshab rje Dar ma rin chen* prepared by Ngawang Gelek Demo Rinpoche from the Tashi Lhunpo redaction (New Delhi: Ngawang Gelek Demo, 1980-1981).

In addition to relying upon these various sources in Sanskrit and Tibetan, we referred to Guiseppe Tucci's incomplete English translation, based primarily on the Sanskrit, and the complete translation, based primarily on Gyaltsab-je's interpretation of the Tibetan, by Jeffrey Hopkins, Lati Rinpoche, and Anne Klein.[1] In general, the best translations evolve through several generations of translators, for each generation benefits from the efforts of earlier translators. This lesson is easily learned from the Tibetans, for in their efforts to accurately translate an enormous body of Sanskrit literature, they often refined their work through several stages of translation. We have taken this to heart in our own work, and by examining earlier renderings, we believe that we have added to the worth of this translation. Although a comparative reading of the translations will show many differences of both style and interpretation, we owe a special thanks to Hopkins and his team. Their earlier work was an inspiration, and in some verses we used words or phrases from their translation, especially when we discovered that we had independently arrived at a nearly identical rendering!

In the course of our work, we encountered several kinds of variations among the extant versions of the text. From a traditional point of view, such variations need not be considered problematic. When traditional Buddhist scholars encounter several versions of a verse, they often feel no need to select one reading as the only "right" one. But for the purposes of translation, we are obliged to make choices, since the body of our text has room for only one version. To give some idea of how we made these choices, we will now briefly discuss the types of variations we encountered and how we dealt with them.

One type of variation stems from the likelihood that some verses in the Tibetan editions are based upon one or more Sanskrit versions that are not represented in the surviving Sanskrit. In such cases, we have favored a Tibetan reading supported by the commentaries, since this translation is intended for use in a Tibetan Buddhist context. At the same time, we have preserved a Sanskritic interpretation in the notes, and we have occasionally suggested emendations that would eliminate the divergence between the Sanskrit and the Tibetan.

In a second type of variation, the available Sanskrit agrees with one of the Tibetan editions, but some of the other Tibetan editions disagree. In this case, we have generally favored an interpretation based upon the reading that is supported by both the available Sanskrit and one of the Tibetan editions, especially if that reading agrees with one or both of the commentaries. In cases of radical divergence, we have mentioned the alternative reading in the notes.

A third type of variation occurs when all of the Tibetan editions agree with the available Sanskrit, but the grammar of the Tibetan translation was construed by the Tibetan commentator Gyaltsab-je in a way that disagrees with the Sanskrit. In some cases, it was possible to be faithful to both the Sanskrit and the Tibetan in a manner that could support Gyaltsab-je's interpretation, but only as a less plausible reading. In those cases, we have favored a straightforward reading of both the Sanskrit and the Tibetan, and we have noted Gyaltsab-je's minor variation in the notes, when necessary. However, in some cases where the available Sanskrit and the Tibetan are in agreement, Gyaltsab-je's construal of the Tibetan grammar leads to an interpretation that can no longer be supported by the Sanskrit, even distantly. Since this translation is primarily for use in a Tibetan Buddhist context, we have generally favored Gyaltsab-je's interpretation in these cases, and we have placed a translation based upon a Sanskritic reading of the Tibetan in the notes.

In keeping with the convention of following the Tibetan line-breaks, we have broken the verses into four lines of verse in English. Strictly speaking, the Sanskrit verses, which are composed in the *anuṣṭubh* meter, consist of two lines each, but each line contains two "feet" (*pāda*) or metrical units. Hence, by breaking the verses into four lines, the Tibetan tradition reflects the presence of four metrical units in each verse. Although we have broken our trans-lation of each verse into four lines also, we have not attempted any imitation of either the Sanskrit or the Tibetan meter. The reader should bear in mind that although the philosophical treatises of ancient India were traditionally composed in verse, they generally were not classified as poetic works (*kāvya*), but rather as doctrinal expressions (*śāstra*) written in verse for ease of memorization. In every instance of the present translation, our aim was to present the clearest possible representation of the meaning of the verse in a manner that still allows for multiple interpretations.

No enterprise such as this can ever truly be thought of as the work of a single individual or team of individuals. Indeed, the persons upon whose wisdom and kindness we have relied are far too numerous to exhaustively list. The present enumeration thus represents just a few of the many gems that comprise the precious garland of our revered teachers, family and friends. First, we thank the great "wish-fulfilling jewel" of the Tibetan people, the monk and spiritual leader Tenzin Gyatso, the Fourteenth Dalai Lama, for his kindness in bestowing these teachings and providing us with the opportunity to translate this work. Second, we express our gratitude for the aid and inspiration of Venerable Geshe Tsultim Gyeltsen. We would also like to acknowledge Gary Schlageter and Geshe-la's other students at Thubten Dhargye Ling, the generous sponsor of this translation.

Many thanks are also due to everyone at Wisdom Publications, especially the publisher Tim McNeill, whose faithfulness and loyalty are a constant inspiration, and the art director Lisa Sawlit, whose eye for beauty and talent for book design continually evoke joy and admiration. Those individuals—be they scribes, translators, or librarians—who have transmitted and preserved this text in its various versions throughout the centuries also deserve our heartfelt thanks. Similarly, we recall with gratitude the efforts of Jñānagarbha, Lui Gyaltsen, Kanakavarman, and Patsub Nyima Drak, whose Tibetan translations and revisions of the *Precious Garland* were indispensable for our own work. Of course, any faults that remain in this translation despite all this assistance are entirely our own.

Finally, we would like to thank a number of other people who helped in the creation of this book in different ways: Tom Burke, Samten Chhosphel, Albert Dalia, Ngawang Jorden, Paul Miller, Masatoshi Nagatomi, Yogesh Panda, John Pettit, Adie Russell, Ngawang Samten, Ngawang Thokmey, and Rām Śānkar Tripāṭhi. Since this list could easily become endless, we will stop here in full recognition that many others deserve our gratitude.

John Dunne and Sara McClintock
March 17, 1997

The Precious Garland

An Epistle to a King

Ācārya Nāgārjuna

Homage to the Three Jewels!
Homage to all buddhas and bodhisattvas!

Chapter One

Elevation and the Highest Good

He is utterly free from all faults
and adorned with all good qualities,
the one friend of all sentient beings —
to that Omniscient One I bow. 1

King, I will explain to you the completely virtuous Dharma[2]
so that you may accomplish it—
for the Dharma will be accomplished (when it is explained)
to a vessel of the true Dharma. 2

That (vessel) first (practices) the Dharma of elevation;
afterwards comes the highest good,
because, having obtained elevation,
one proceeds in stages to the highest good. 3

Here, (we) maintain that elevation is happiness,
and the highest good is liberation.
In brief, the method for (attaining) them
I summarize as faith and wisdom. 4

Because one has faith, one partakes of the Dharma;
because one has wisdom, one truly understands;
of these two, wisdom is the foremost,
but faith is the one that must come first. 5

One who does not discount the Dharma

through desire, anger, fear, or confusion
should be known as one with faith —
a supreme vessel of the highest good. 6

A wise (person) is one who,
having accurately analyzed
all actions of body, speech, and mind,
always acts for the benefit of self and others. 7

Refraining from violence and from theft,
not engaging in adultery;
restraining from lying, divisive speech,
harsh words, and idle talk; 8

abandoning miserliness, maliciousness,
and nihilistic views —
These are the ten bright paths of action.
The ten dark ones are the opposite. 9

In brief Dharma consists of not drinking liquor,
maintaining a proper occupation,
abandoning harm, being respectfully generous,
honoring the worthy, and (cultivating) love. 10

Dharma does not come about merely
through engaging in physical austerities;
through that (type of practice) one neither ceases harming others,
nor does one benefit them. 11

One who does not respect the great path of the true Dharma
with its manifest generosity, ethics, and tolerance,
follows the mistaken path of inflicting hardship on the body
just as (a cow in a herd follows) the line of cattle (in front).[3] 12

Such a person, with a body entwined[4] by
the savage snakes[5] of negative mental states,
wanders for a very long time in the terrifying wilderness
of cyclic existence, whose trees are limitless beings. 13

Due to murder one is born with a short life-span;
due to violence one encounters much torment;
due to stealing one becomes impoverished;
due to adultery one has enemies. 14

By telling lies one becomes reviled;
Through speaking divisively, one loses friends;
due to speaking harshly, one hears unpleasant noises;
From engaging in idle gossip, one's words will be disregarded. 15

Covetousness destroys one's desired objects;
maliciousness is said to bestow fear;
wrong views lead to evil worldviews;
imbibing liquor brings mental confusion. 16

Through not giving gifts one gets poverty;
wrong livelihood results in getting tricked;
arrogance leads to a lowly station;
jealousy brings about homeliness. 17

From anger comes a bad complexion,
and stupidity, since one will not question the wise.
These are the effects when one is (reborn as) a human,
but prior to all of them there is a bad rebirth. 18

Such are widely known to be the ripened results
of these (actions) which are called "the nonvirtues."
For all of the virtuous actions

there are the opposite effects. 19

Greed, hatred, and confusion, and the karma
that arises from them are nonvirtuous.
Nongreed, nonhatred, and nonconfusion,
and the karma that arises from them are virtuous. 20

From nonvirtue comes all suffering,
likewise all negative rebirths.
From virtue comes all positive rebirths,
and the happiness within all births. 21

This Dharma[6] is considered to be twofold:
one should not engage in nonvirtue
through mind, body or speech,
but one should always engage in virtue (through those three). 22

Through this Dharma one is freed from (rebirth as)
a hell being, hungry ghost, or animal.
As a human or celestial being one obtains
all happiness, glory, and sovereignty. 23

And through the concentrations, immeasurables, and formless (absorptions),
one experiences the pleasure of Brahmā and so on.
Such, in summary, is the Dharma
of elevation and its results. 24

But the Victors said that
the Dharma of the highest good
is the subtle and profoundly appearing;[7]
it is frightening to unlearned, childish beings. 25

"I am not, nor will I be.
There is nothing that is mine, nor will there be."
Stated thus, (the teaching of selflessness) terrifies the childish.
For the wise, it puts an end to fear. 26

All "beings" arise from fixation on self
such that they (thereby) are fixated on "mine";
this is what has been stated
by the one who speaks solely for the sake of beings. 27

Ultimately, the notions "I exist" and
"What is mine exists" are false, because
from the perspective of knowing (things)
as they truly are, there is neither ("I" nor "mine"). 28

The aggregates[8] arise from fixation on "I";
the fixation on "I" is ultimately unreal.
How then can there really be any production
of that whose seed is unreal? 29

Seeing in this way that the aggregates
are unreal, one forsakes fixation on "I."
And due to forsaking the fixation on "I,"
the (afflicted) aggregates do not arise again. 30

Depending upon a mirror,
the reflection of one's face
is seen, but it does not
ultimately exist at all. 31

Likewise, depending on the aggregates
fixation on the "I" is perceived;
but that ("I") does not exist truly,

just like the reflection of one's face. 32

Without depending on the mirror
the reflection of one's face is not seen.
Likewise, without depending on the aggregates,
there is no (notion of an) "I." 33

Having heard this kind of topic (emptiness),
the Superior Ānanda obtained the Dharma-eye.
Then he himself taught (that topic)
repeatedly to the monks and nuns.[9] 34

As long as one is fixated on the aggregates,
one will also be fixated on "I" with regard to them.
If one is fixated on "I," karma (will be committed) again,
and due to that (karma) one will again be reborn. 35

With these three phases mutually causing each other,
the circle of saṃsāra whirls around,
like the circle (formed by a whirling) torch,
without beginning, middle or end. 36

But that (samsaric process) is not attained from itself,
from something else, or from both; nor is it attained in the three times.
Therefore, (for one who knows this) the fixation on "I" ceases,
and hence also karma and birth. 37

Seeing in this fashion the arisal of effect from cause
and also seeing its cessation,
(the wise) think, "The world is ultimately
neither existent nor nonexistent." 38

Having listened to this Dharma

that puts an end to suffering,
the undiscerning, afraid of the fearless state,
are terrified because they do not understand.[10] 39

You are not afraid (about the claim that)
all this will not exist in nirvāṇa;
why then are you afraid when told that here
that (threefold process of saṃsāra) does not exist? 40

In liberation there is neither Self nor aggregates;
if you are intent[11] upon that kind of liberation,
why are you not pleased with (the teaching that)
refutes Self and aggregates here as well? 41

Nirvāṇa is not even nonexistent,
so how could it be existent?
Nirvāṇa is said to be the cessation
of the notions of existence and nonexistence. 42

In brief, a nihilistic view
is the belief that karma has no effect.
It is nonmeritorious, and (it leads to) low rebirth;
it is said to be a false view. 43

In brief, a realist view
is the belief that karma has an effect.
It is meritorious, and it leads to high rebirth;
it is said that it is a proper view. 44

Through knowledge, one subdues the (notions of) existence
and nonexistence, and one thus transcends sin and merit.
Hence, one is liberated from high and low rebirths—
this is what the holy one says.[12] 45

Seeing that production has a cause,
one transcends (the notion) of nonexistence.
Seeing that cessation has a cause,
one does not accept (the notion of) existence. 46

A cause that occurs before (its effect) or simultaneously (with it)
is not really a cause at all,
because (such causes) are not accepted conceptually,
and production is not accepted ultimately.[13] 47

When there is this, that arises,
just as when there is "long," there is "short."
When this is produced, that arises,
just as, when a lamp's (flame) is produced, light arises. 48

But when there is no short,
there is no intrinsically existent long.
And when a lamp's (flame) is not produced,
the light also does not arise.[14] 49

Seeing that an effect arises from a cause,
one does not claim that (causality) is nonexistent,
having provisionally accepted (causality) in accord with
the way it arises for the world from conceptual fabrication.[15] 50

(Ultimate causality is) refuted; it would be absolutistic
to accept that it has not arisen from conceptual fabrication
and that it is truly real, just as it is. (But its ultimate reality) is not (accepted).
Thus, not relying on the two (extremes), one is liberated.[16] 51

A form that is viewed from afar
is seen clearly by those nearby;

if a mirage were actually water,
why would those nearby not see it? 52

As in the case of a mirage,
those far away who (view) the world
see it to be real just as it is,
but being signless, it is not seen by those nearby 53

A mirage seems to be water,
but it is not water, nor is it real.
Likewise, the aggregates seem to be the Self,
but they are not the Self, nor are they even real. 54

(Seeing) a mirage, one might think,
"That is water," and then go up to it;
if one still grasped (at the water, thinking,)
"That water isn't here," it would be quite stupid. 55

Likewise, it is confused
to apprehend this mirage-like world
as either "existent" or "nonexistent."
If confused, one will not obtain liberation. 56

The nihilist goes to a low rebirth;
the realist attains a high rebirth;
but through knowing (reality) just as it is,
not relying on the two (extremes), one is liberated. 57

Asserting neither existence nor nonexistence
By knowing (reality) just as it is,
(if) one would thereby be a nihilist,
why would one not also be a realist? 58

If the refutation of existence
were to entail nihilism by implication,
then why is realism not entailed
by the refutation of nonexistence? 59

(Buddhists) do not actually assert nihilism,
nor behave nihilistically; and, because
they rely on awakening, they do not think as nihilists;
so how can they be called nihilists? 60

Ask the worldly (philosophers, such as) the Sāṃkhyas, Vaiśeṣikas,
and Jains, who assert (the real existence) of the person
and aggregates, whether they maintain that (the interdependent is)
beyond existence and nonexistence.[17] 61

Realize, therefore, that the nectar of the Buddhas' teaching,
which is beyond all (notions of) "existence" and "nonexistence,"
and which is called "the profound,"
is (our) unique Dharma-inheritance.[18] 62

The world does not go out of existence,
nor come (into existence); it does not remain
for even an instant; it has a nature beyond
the three times, so how could it be real? 63

Ultimately, the world and nirvāṇa do not come (into existence),
nor do they go (out of existence), nor do they remain (existent).
So what kind of distinction could there really be
between the world and nirvāṇa? 64

Since remaining (existent) does not (really) occur,
ultimately, there is neither production nor cessation;
How can (something) be ultimately "produced,"

or "ceased," or "remaining existent?" 65

If there is constant transformation,
how could real things be non-momentary?
And if there were not transformation,
how could there really be any change? 66

(Something is) momentary because
it either ceases partially or entirely.
Neither of these two (possibilities) makes sense
because a difference is not perceived. 67

If (a real thing) is momentary, then since it would cease to exist
entirely (at each moment), how could anything be old?
And if (a real thing) is nonmomentary, then since it would
persist (without change), how could anything be old? 68

Just as one conceives of a moment as having an end,
so too one should conceive of it as having a beginning and middle;
since a moment has a threefold (temporal) nature,
the world does not remain for (even) a moment.[19] 69

As with a moment, one should also consider
the (tripartite nature of its) beginning, middle and end.
There is no beginning, middle or end
(that arises) either from itself or something else. 70

No (material thing) is a unitary whole, because it has
many directional parts;
and there is no (material thing) that does not have directional parts.
Without the unitary whole, there cannot be the many (parts)—
without the existent, there cannot be the nonexistent. 71

The existent becomes nonexistent because
it either ceases (on its own) or is counteracted (by something else).
But since the "existent" is impossible,
how could there be (its) cessation or counteragent? 72

Therefore, ultimately, the world is not lessened
by (someone) attaining nirvāṇa.
When asked whether there is any end to the world,
the Victor remained silent. 73

The wise understand that
the Omniscient One is indeed omniscient
because he did not teach the profound Dharmas
to beings who were not (suitable) vessels. 74

Thus, the all-seeing, complete buddhas
have said that the Dharma of the highest good
is profound, devoid of grasping,
and also without any foundation.[20] 75

But persons who delight in foundations,
not having transcended (notions of) "existence"
and "nonexistence,"
are terrified by this foundationless Dharma,
and, being unskilled, they are devastated. 76

Terrified of that fearless state,
devastated, they lead others to devastation.
See to it, O king, that no matter what,
you are not led to devastation by those already devastated. 77

King, so that you might not be devastated,
I will explain in accord with the scriptures

this correct, transcendent approach,
that does not rely on the two (extremes)— 78

Beyond both sin and merit, it is the profound meaning
derived (from the scriptures); other (philosophers, such as) the
Tīrthikas,[21] and even some of our own have not tasted it,
for they fear the foundationless. 79

The "person" is not earth,
nor water, fire, wind or space.
Nor is it consciousness; and if it is not all of these (together),
what other thing could the "person" be? 80

The "person" is not truly real
because it is composed of the six constituents.[22]
Likewise, since each of the constituents is also
composed (of parts), they are not truly real. 81

The aggregates are not the Self, nor do they exist in the (Self);
Nor is the (Self) in the (aggregates), but without them, the (Self) cannot exist.
And the Self and aggregates are not intermingled, as with fire and fuel.
Therefore, how could the Self exist? 82

The (other) three elements are not earth, nor are they in earth;
nor is the (earth) in them, but without them, the (earth element) cannot exist.
Such is also the case for each (of the other elements).
Therefore, as with the Self, the elements[23] are unreal. 83

Earth, water, fire and wind
are each not essentially existent,
since[24] each one does not exist without the (other) three,

and the (other) three do not exist without each one. 84

If each does not exist without (the other) three,
and (the other) three do not exist without each one,
then they individually do not essentially exist,
so how could they arise as a compound? 85

If each (element) exists on its own,
then why would fire not occur without fuel?
Likewise, why would there not be water, wind and earth
without fluctuation, resistance and coherence? 86

If you claim that (only) fire is well known (to depend on fuel),
then, according to you, how could the other three be independent?
It does not make sense for those three to be
incompatible with what is interdependently arisen.[25] 87

(If) those (elements) each exist on their own,
how could they exist mutually?
And (if they) do not each exist on their own,
how could they exist mutually? 88

If each does not exist on its own,
but wherever there is one, the remaining (three are present),
then (if) not mingled, they cannot be present in one locus,
and (if) commingled, they cannot each exist on their own. 89

How can elements that do not exist on their own
have any intrinsic characteristics? (And when commingled,
one element) cannot predominate (since it) does not exist on its own;
(hence, their) characteristics are stated conventionally.[26] 90

This approach also applies to colors, odors,

tastes, and tactile (objects). Such is also the case
with eye (faculty), consciousness, and form,
ignorance, karma and birth,
Agent, patient[27] and action, also number,
conjunction, cause and effect, and time,
long and short, and so on—
designation and designated. 91–92

The Sage has stated that
earth, water, fire and wind,
short and long, subtle and coarse, virtue and so on
cease in the awareness (of the ultimate). 93

Earth, water, fire and wind
cannot find any place (to exist)
in that undisclosable, limitless,[28]
fully sovereign awareness. 94

Short and long, subtle and coarse,
virtue and nonvirtue,
and also name and form,
all cease in this (awareness). 95

All which previously appeared in awareness
due to that which was not known,
later will likewise cease in awareness
because one has come to know (just) that. 96

It is maintained that all beings and (their) qualities
are the fuel for the fire of awareness.
Having been incinerated by brilliant
true analysis, they are (all) pacified. 97

Later, when one has ascertained suchness,
if what was previously constructed by ignorance
does not maintain its existence,
then how could there be nonexistence?[29] 98

Since it is merely the absence of form,
space is merely a designation.
How can there be form without the elements?
Therefore, (form) is also a mere designation.[30] 99

One should consider sensation, recognition,
mental conditioning and consciousness
in the manner (that one considered) the elements and Self.
Hence, the six constituents are selfless. 100

Chapter Two

Combination (of Elevation and the Highest Good)

When one splits apart the plantain tree
along with all its parts, (one finds) no (core) at all;
so too, when one 'splits apart' the person
with its six constituents, (one finds) no (essence) at all. 1

Hence, the Victors have said
that all things are selfless;
it has been demonstrated to you
that all the six constituents are selfless.[31] 2

In this way, neither Self nor non-Self
are ultimately perceived just as they are.
Therefore, the Great Sage refuted
both the belief in Self and in non-Self. 3

As for what one sees, hears, and so on,
the Sage did not call them either real or unreal,
because by (holding) a thesis, (one implies its) antithesis.
Thus, neither is ultimately real. 4

Hence, this world is ultimately
beyond (being) real or unreal.
Therefore, (the Buddha) does not ultimately accept
(the notions that) "It is" or "It is not." 5

How could the Omniscient One

say that what (he knows to be)
utterly nonexistent is finite or infinite,
both or neither? 6

There have been innumerable past buddhas;
likewise, future buddhas and present buddhas are innumerable.
And the extent of the three times' sentient beings
is considered to be billions of times more (than those buddhas).[32] 7

The world's cessation, occurring in the three times,
does not cause its increase.
Why then did the Omniscient One
(maintain that) its beginning and end is indeterminate?[33] 8

Such is the profound Dharma
that is obscure to ordinary beings;
that the world is like an illusion
is the ambrosia of the buddhas' teaching. 9

An elephant created through magical illusion
might seem to arise and cease,
but ultimately there is not
any arisal or cessation at all. 10

So too, the world, like a magical illusion,
might seem to arise and cease,
but ultimately there is not
any arisal and cessation at all. 11

An illusory elephant does not come
from anywhere, nor go anywhere;
since it is merely (a manifestation of) mental confusion,
it does not ultimately exist. 12

So too, the world, like a magical illusion,
does not come from anywhere, nor go anywhere;
since it is merely (a manifestation of) mental confusion,
it does not ultimately exist. 13

The nature of the world transcends all three times;
except for (being designated in) conventional terms,
how could it be ultimately
either "existent" or "nonexistent"? 14

For this reason and no other,
the Buddha said that (the world)
was indeterminate with regard to four aspects—
being finite or infinite, dual or nondual. 15

The impurity of the body is obvious—
it is an object of direct perception;
although one sees it constantly,
it does not remain in one's mind. 16

If that is the case, then how could this
extremely subtle, profound, and unlocated
holy Dharma, which is not directly perceptible,
easily enter into one's mind? 17

Hence, having attained awakening, the Sage realized
that since this Dharma was so profound,
people would not understand it;
so he refrained from teaching the Dharma. 18

If this Dharma is misunderstood,
it will devastate the unwise,
for they will sink deeply into

the filth of nihilistic views. 19

And from misunderstanding this (Dharma),
fools who presume themselves pundits,
ruined by their denial of it,
plummet straight down to Avīci hell. 20

Through eating poor food,
one will come to ruin;
but by eating the right food,
one attains vigor, health, strength and pleasure. 21

Likewise, through poor understanding,
one will come to ruin.
But through right understanding,
one attains happiness and unexcelled awakening. 22

Therefore, do not deny this (Dharma),
and abandon nihilistic views;
in order to obtain all aims,
strive for perfect understanding. 23

When this Dharma is not understood,
the fixation on "I" continues.
Due to that, (one engages) in positive and negative karma,
and from that come positive and negative rebirths. 24

Therefore, as long as you have not understood
this Dharma that destroys the fixation on "I,"
devote yourself to the Dharma
of giving, morality and patience. 25

King, if you undertake deeds that

begin with Dharma, have Dharma
in the middle and Dharma at the end,
you will not despair in this world or the next. 26

Through Dharma you attain fame and pleasure,
you have no fear now nor at death;
and in the next world, you will have great joy—
so devote yourself always to Dharma. 27

Dharma is the highest policy;[34]
Dharma pleases the world;
and if the world is pleased,
you will not be deceived here or hereafter. 28

But a policy that proceeds without Dharma
will not please the world
And if the world is not pleased,
you will not be happy here or hereafter. 29

A useless (political) theory
is one that intends to deceive others;
it is harsh and a path to bad rebirths—
how could the unwise make such a theory useful? 30

Since that (deception) will just deceive one
for many thousands of rebirths,
how could one intent on deceiving others
be a true 'statesman' at all? 31

If you wish to make your foes unhappy,
do away with your faults, and enhance your good qualities.
That way, you will gain great benefit,
and your enemies will also be displeased. 32

Be generous, speak gently, be beneficent;
act with the same intention (as you expect of others);
through these (ways of acting), bring together the world,
and also sustain the Dharma. 33

A single truth (uttered) by kings
makes (their subjects) have firm trust in them.
Likewise, one falsehood on their part
is the best way to lose that trust. 34

(To speak) the truth is (to speak in a manner) that is not deceptive;
it is not what is in fact distorted by an intention.
(A statement) is true by being only of benefit to others;
the other (kind of statement) is false, since it is not beneficial.[35] 35

A single, shining act of generosity
hides the flaws of a king;
likewise, an instance of greed
will contradict all of his good qualities. 36

It is profound to be tranquil;
and for its profundity, tranquillity is highly respected.
From respect come glory and authority.
Therefore, devote yourself to tranquillity. 37

By being wise, your mind will not waver;
not dependent on the opinions of others,
you will be steadfast, king, and not deceived.
Therefore, devote yourself to wisdom. 38

Truth, generosity, tranquillity and wisdom—
a king who has these four excellent qualities
will be praised by gods and humans

just like these four excellent Dharmas. 39

Wisdom and Dharma always increase
in (a king) who consults with those who are
restrained in speech and pure,
and possess undefiled wisdom and compassion. 40

Those who speak beneficially are rare.
Even more rare are those who listen.
And more rare yet than these are those who
quickly implement something beneficial.[36] 41

Having realized that something beneficial is unpleasant,
you should quickly put it into practice,
just as a prudent[37] person, in order to become healthy,
takes his medication, even though it is noxious. 42

You should always reflect upon
the impermanence of life, health and political power.
That way you will with true effort
strive uniquely (to practice this) Dharma. 43

Seeing that you will definitely die,
and that, when dead, you suffer from your negativity,
you should not engage in any negativity
even for the sake of temporary pleasures. 44

In some cases, the dire (result of negativity) is not observed;
in other instances, the dire (result) is observed.
If you have confidence in the (former) case,
why are you not concerned about the other? 45

From intoxicants come the world's disdain,

your own failure and loss of your wealth.
Confused, you do what you should not.
Therefore, always refrain from intoxicants. 46

Gambling causes attachment, dislike, and anger,
deception, trickery and an occasion for wildness,
lying, pointless chatter, and harsh speech.
Therefore, always refrain from gambling. 47

Most attachment to women comes from
the belief that women's bodies are pure.
But in actuality there is no purity
in a woman's body at all. 48

Her mouth is a vessel of impurity,
with putrid saliva and gunk between her teeth;
Her nose is a pot of snot, phlegm and mucous,
and her eyes contain eye-slime and tears. 49

Her torso is a container of excrement,
holding urine, the lungs, liver and such.
The confused do not see that a woman is such;
thus, they lust after her body. 50

Like unknowing persons, who have become attached
to an ornamented vessel filled with filth,
Unknowing and confused worldly beings
are attached to women.[38] 50a

If the world is greatly attached
to the noxious objects that are bodies,
which should cause non-attachment,
how then can it be led to non-attachment? 51

Just as filth-loving pigs[39] are greatly attached
to heaps[40] of feces and urine,
so too the filth-loving pigs that are desirous people
are greatly attached to heaps of feces and urine. 52

Foolish persons imagine
that this city (of bugs) that is the body,
with cavities that are sources of filth,
is something conducive to pleasure. 53

When you yourself see the impurities
of excrement, urine and such,
how can the body, being composed of them,
be something pleasant for you? 54

It is produced by a seed of impure essence,
an admixture of ovum and semen.
How can the lustful be attached to it
when they know its nature is impure? 55

One who lies with this filthy mass,
covered with skin moistened by those fluids,
is doing nothing more than lying
on top of a woman's bladder. 56

Whether it be beautiful or ugly,
whether it be young or old,
the body of any woman is filthy,
so to what special quality could you be attached? 57

It is not right to yearn for
a pile of excrement, even if it has a nice color
or is very fresh or nicely shaped;

likewise, one should not yearn for a woman's body. 58

While the nature of this rotting corpse,
with its putrid core covered with skin,
looks extremely terrible,
why (do the lustful) not see it? 59

"The skin is not impure;
it is just like a soft cloth."
Like a leather bag filled with a turd,
how could it be clean? 60

While a vase filled with excrement
might glitter, it is still objectionable.
The body, whose nature is filth,
is filled with filth; why is it not objectionable? 61

If you object to excrement,
why not object to this body which takes
pure perfume, garlands, food and drink
and turns them into filth? 62

A pile of excrement is objectionable,
whether it be from you or someone else;
why not then object to these filthy bodies,
whether your own or someone else's? 63

Your own body is just as filthy
as the body of a woman.
So doesn't it make sense
to be non-attached to both the external and internal? 64

Even though you daily rinse off

the excretions from your "nine wounds,"
if you still do not realize that the body is impure,
then what is the point of explaining this to you? 65

Some compose erotic poetry
about this filthy body—
O, what shamelessness! What idiocy!
How worthy of people's contempt! 66

In this (world), sentient beings,
obscured by the darkness of unknowing,
mostly quarrel about what they lust for,
like dogs fighting over filth. 67

If you scratch an itch, it feels good,
but it feels even better to have no itch at all.
So too, one is happy in obtaining worldly desires,
but there is greater happiness in having no desires at all. 68

When you analyze things in this fashion,
even if you are not yet freed from desires,
you will cease lusting after women
through the gradual decrease of your desire. 69

Hunting is the terrible cause
of a short life, fear, and suffering,
and also rebirth in the hells. Therefore,
always refrain firmly from killing. 70

Like a snake all smeared with filth,
poison dripping from its fangs,
despicable[41] indeed is the one
on account of whom others feel terror. 71

When a great rain cloud appears,
farmers experience much joy;
excellent in this way is the one
on account of whom beings feel joy. 72

Therefore, refrain from what is not Dharma.
Heedfully practice the Dharma. 73ab

If you and the world wish
to attain unexcelled awakening,
its roots are *bodhicitta* that is
as firm as the king of mountains,[42]
compassion that is as vast as space,
and the wisdom that relies not on duality. 73cd–74

Great king, listen now to the way
that your body will be adorned
with the thirty-two distinctive marks
that indicate a great being. 75

Due to honoring *caitya*[43] and those who are worthy,
the Superiors and also the Elders,
your glorious hands and feet will be wheel-marked,
showing that you shall turn the wheel.[44] 76

King, always be steadfast
in your commitments concerning the Dharma.
That way, you shall become a bodhisattva
who has level and even feet. 77

Through generosity and gentle speech,
and by acting beneficently and consistently,
you will have hands with lines

joined by glorious finger-webs. 78

Through abundantly giving the best food and drink,
your glorious hands and feet will be soft,
and you will have a large body
with seven broadly curving parts.[45] 79

Through renouncing violence and freeing those to be killed,
your body will be beautiful, straight and tall.
You will have a long life, your digits will be long,
and your heels will be broad. 80

Through enhancing the practices that you have undertaken,
you will be glorious, you will have a good complexion;
your ankles will not be prominent,
and you will be marked with body hairs that curl upward. 81

By both learning and imparting with respect
the sciences, crafts and other fields of knowledge,
you will have the calves of an antelope,
and be quick-witted with great wisdom. 82

Through the avowed practice of quickly giving
your wealth at the request of others,
your arms will be broad and facile,
and you will be a leader of the world. 83

Through seeing to the reconciliation
of friends and relatives who have had a falling out,
you will be a holy person
with secret organ retracted into the abdomen. 84

By giving pleasant and excellent

palatial dwellings adorned with carpets,
your skin will have a gentle hue
like refined, untarnished gold. 85

Through giving unexcelled authority
and properly following your guru,
your resplendent body hairs will grow one by one,
and your face will be adorned with the forehead curl. 86

By speaking gently and pleasingly
and acting in accord with the well spoken,
your shoulders will be well rounded
and you will have a leonine upper body. 87

Through serving and healing the sick,
you will have a broad back,
you will be imperturbable
and all tastes will be supreme. 88

By focusing on deeds that accord with Dharma,
you will have an *uṣṇīṣa*[46] on your head,
and your body will also have
the symmetry of a banyan tree. 89

Having spoken truthful and gentle words
for a long period of time,
you will have a broad tongue, liege,
and your speech will be a Brahmā's sound. 90

Through always and continually
uttering words that are true,
you will have a lion's jaw;
glorious, you will be undefeatable. 91

Through behaving with respect and service
in an appropriate manner,
your teeth will be very white,
and lustrous; they will also be even. 92

Having become accustomed to words
that are true and not divisive,[47]
you will have glorious teeth, forty in number,
set closely together and excellent. 93

From gazing on sentient beings with love,
without attachment, aversion or confusion,
your eyes will be sparkling blue
with eyelashes like a cow. 94

Thus, you should recognize
that these are, in brief,
the thirty-two marks that indicate
a great, lion-like person. 95

The eighty secondary signs
have love as their concordant cause.
But concerned that this treatise will be too long,
I will not explain them to you, king. 96

Although all wheel-turning monarchs
have these (marks and secondary signs),
their purity, beauty and luster
cannot compare with a buddha's. 97

Each of the marks and signs
of a wheel-turning monarch
are said to come from one cause—

clear faith in the King of Sages. 98

But even were such virtue to be
uniquely amassed over a billion eons,
it would not be sufficient to produce
even a single pore of a buddha. 99

The brilliance of the suns
has some slight similarity to a firefly;
likewise, the marks of the buddhas
are slightly similar to those of the wheel-turning monarchs. 100

Chapter Three

The Collections for Awakening

Great King, listen to the way in which
the marks of a buddha
arise from an inconceivable amount of merit
according to the great Mahāyāna scriptures. 1

A single pore of a buddha is made
from ten times the following amount of merit—
the total merit from which all Pratyekabuddhas have arisen,
the total merit that has produced all learners and those beyond learning,
and the total merit of the entire universe,
which, like the universe, is infinite.
Each pore of a buddha likewise
arises from that much merit. 2–3

A single secondary sign of a buddha
is obtained through one hundred times
the amount of merit needed
to produce all of a buddha's pores. 4

King, that amount of merit
completes one auspicious secondary sign;
likewise, from that amount of merit
arises each of them up to eighty. 5

A single mark of a great person

comes from one hundred times
the mass of merit needed
to produce all eighty secondary signs. 6

Through a thousand times the vast merit
which causes thirty of the marks,
arises like the full moon
the swirl of hair between the brows. 7

From a hundred thousand times the merit
required for the forehead swirl
is produced the protector's *uṣṇīṣa*
the top of which is imperceptible. 8

You should realize that a single Dharma-conch
of the One who Possesses the Ten Powers
arises from the amount of merit that produces the *uṣṇīṣa*
multiplied a million ten millions of times.[48] 8a

Thus, even though the merit is limitless
it is merely said to have a limit,
just as one expresses all the regions of the universe
by subsuming them in the ten (directions). 9

If the causes of a buddha's form-body
are immeasurable, like the universe,
how then could the causes
of the Dharma-body be measurable? 10

If in all cases a vast effect arises from a small cause,
then one should cease to believe
that a measurable effect comes from
the immeasurable causes of buddhahood. 11

In brief, King, the buddhas' form-bodies
arise from the collection of merit,
and their dharma-body is born
from the collection of wisdom. 12

Thus, these two collections
cause the obtainment of buddhahood;
hence, in short, devote yourself
always to merit and wisdom. 13

You should not be discouraged about
(accumulating) the merit for obtaining awakening,
since there are reasons to be reassured
set forth by both reasoning and scripture. 14

In all regions, space, earth, water,
fire and vital energy are infinite;
so too it is acknowledged
that suffering sentient beings are infinite. 15

Through a bodhisattva's love and compassion
those infinite sentient beings
are led out of their suffering
and definitely brought to buddhahood. 16

Since sentient beings are infinite,
from the point that this commitment is made,
one who remains resolute
whether s/he is asleep or awake,
or even careless, will still constantly gather
merit that, like beings, is infinite.
And since this merit is infinite, it is said
that attaining infinite buddhahood is not hard. 17–18

Remaining for an infinite time
and wishing to obtain infinite awakening
for the sake of infinite beings,
the (bodhisattva) performs infinite virtue,
so how could s/he not obtain before long
awakening, even though it be infinite,
through the collection of these four[49] that are infinite? 19–20

What is called "infinite merit"
and also that called "infinite wisdom"
quickly eradicate the suffering
of both body and mind. 21

Hunger, thirst and other such physical suffering
occurs in negative rebirths due to one's negativity.
The (bodhisattva) does not engage in negativity;
due to merit, s/he has no such suffering in other rebirths. 22

Due to confusion comes the mental suffering
of attachment, anger, fear, lust and such.
The (bodhisattva) quickly eliminates this (suffering)
by realizing that (all things) are foundationless. 23

If (the bodhisattva) is not greatly harmed
by mental and physical pain, then even though
in an endless universe s/he leads the world,
why would s/he be discouraged? 24

Even brief suffering is difficult to bear—
what need then to mention suffering for long?
But even if infinite in duration, what could harm
one who has no suffering and is happy? 25

The (bodhisattva) has no physical suffering—
how could s/he have mental suffering?
But through compassion, s/he feels pain for the world;
for that reason, s/he remains for a long time. 26

Thus, do not be discouraged by thinking
that buddhahood is so distant.
Always be assiduous in this (practice)
to eliminate faults and obtain good qualities. 27

Recognizing that they are flawed,
abandon attachment, anger and confusion.
Realizing that they are good qualities, devote yourself
respectfully to non-attachment, non-anger and non-confusion. 28

Through attachment, you go to the realm of hungry ghosts.
Due to anger, your are pitched into hell.
Out of confusion, you are reborn as an animal.
Through their opposites, you become a human or celestial. 29

Eliminating faults and acquiring good qualities
is the Dharma for one seeking elevation.
The elimination of all grasping by means of knowledge
is the Dharma for one seeking the highest good. 30

In a respectful manner, make buddha-images,
stūpas and vast temples,
providing extensive and excellent
chambers and so on. 31

From all kinds of precious substances,
please make well drawn,
beautifully proportioned images

of buddhas seated upon lotus flowers.[50] 32

With every possible effort take care of
the holy Dharma and the community of monks and nuns.
Adorn the *stūpas* with gold
and with lattices made from gems. 33

Honor the *stūpas* with offerings
of gold and silver flowers,
diamonds, coral, and pearls,
sapphires, lapis lazuli and emeralds. 34

To honor those who teach the holy Dharma,
with goods and with services,
do what brings them joy and respectfully
devote yourself to the six Dharmas. 35

Serve your gurus and listen respectfully;
aid them and attend upon them.
Always respectfully honor
(other) bodhisattvas as well. 36

You should not pay such respect,
honor or homage to others, who are Tīrthikas.[51]
Through that (misplaced respect), the unknowing
become attached to faulty (teachers). 37

Offer manuscripts and volumes
of the sayings of the King of Sages
and the treatises that come from those sayings,
along with their prerequisites, pens and ink. 38

For the sake of increasing wisdom,

provide for the livelihood of the schoolmasters
in all the educational institutions of the land
and formally[52] grant estates to them. 39

With (the proceeds from) your fields
establish wages for doctors and barbers
for the sake of the elderly, the young and the ill
so as to relieve the sufferings of sentient beings. 40

You of good wisdom, establish rest houses
and build parks and causeways,
pools, pavilions[53] and cisterns;
provide for bedding, grasses and wood. 41

Build pavilions in all towns,
at temples and in all cities.
Along any thoroughfare where
water is scarce, provide cisterns. 42

Out of your compassion, always care for
the ill, the homeless, those afflicted by suffering
and the downtrodden and unfortunate.
Respectfully apply yourself to aiding them. 43

It is not proper for you to partake
of seasonal foods and beverages, produce,
grain and fruits, until you have offered them
to monks and nuns and those asking for alms. 44

At the sites of cisterns place
shoes, parasols, and water filters,
tweezers for removing thorns,
needles, thread and fans. 45

At the cisterns also place the three kinds
of fruit, the three kinds of salt,
honey, eye-medicine and antidotes to poison.
Also write formulas for medicinal treatments and spells. 46

At the cisterns also place ointments
for the body, feet and head,
cradles, ladles and ewers,
brass pots, axes and so on. 47

In cool, shady spots make small cisterns
filled with potable water
and provided with sesame, rice,
grain, foods and molasses.[54] 48

At the openings of anthills
have trustworthy persons
constantly place food and water,
molasses and piles of grain. 49

Both before and after each meal
always offer in a pleasant manner
food to hungry ghosts,
dogs, ants, birds and so on. 50

Always care extensively for (places) in the world
that are oppressed or where crops have failed;
that have suffered harm or where there is plague
or that have been conquered (in war). 51

Provide seeds and food to farmers
who have fallen on hard times.
Eliminate excessive taxes

and reduce the portion (of products taxed). 52

Protect (citizens) from debt;
eliminate (new) tolls and reduce (excessive) tolls.
Eliminate the suffering of those
who wait at your door (with their petitions unanswered). 53

Eliminate bandits in your own land
and in other lands as well.
Keep prices level
and place the proper value (on goods). 54

Be thoroughly familiar
with all that your advisors say,
and always do whatever
is healthy for the world. 55

Just as you pay attention to
whatever you think will benefit you,
so too pay attention to
what you think will benefit others. 56

Like the earth, water, fire and wind,
wild herbs and the plants of the forest,
make yourself (and possessions) available
for the general enjoyment (of all). 57

Even when taking their seventh step,[55]
bodhisattvas have the attitude of giving away
all their possessions; this produces merit in them
that is as limitless as the sky itself. 58

If you bestow well adorned, beautiful maidens

upon those that seek them,
you will thereby attain
the *dhāraṇīs*[56] that hold the holy Dharma. 59

Previously the Victor bestowed
eighty thousand maidens adorned
with all kinds of ornaments
accompanied by all kinds of goods. 60

To those who come begging, lovingly give
numerous and resplendent clothes,
ornaments, perfumes and garlands,
and other objects of enjoyment. 61

There is no greater act of generosity
than to grant to the extremely unfortunate
who are bereft of some aspect of the Dharma
the happy chance[57] (to receive teachings on it). 62

You should even give poison to those
for whom poison would be beneficial.
But if even the best food will not help someone,
you should not give it to them. 63

It is said that if a snake has bitten it,
it is helpful to cut off one's finger.
Likewise, the Sage said that if it benefits others,
one should even do something unpleasant. 64

Have supreme respect for the holy Dharma
and those who teach the Dharma.
Respectfully listen to the Dharma
and offer the Dharma (to others). 65

Do not revel in worldly discourse;
take delight in the transcendent.
Just as you develop good qualities in yourself,
develop them also in others. 66

Do not be satisfied with the Dharma you have heard;
keep in mind its meaning and analyze it.
Always respectfully offer
a gift of thanksgiving to your gurus. 67

Do not study profane (philosophical systems), such as
that of the Cārvākas. Give up debate that is for the sake of pride.
Do not speak in praise of your own good qualities,
but rather speak of even your enemies' good qualities. 68

Do not attack what is vital (to another),[58]
nor make statements with
a negative attitude toward others.
Instead, examine your own errors. 69

You should eliminate in yourself those faults
that the wise always decry in others.
And to the best of your ability,[59]
eliminate them in others as well. 70

Do not be angry when others do harm,
but realize that it is (the effect of) previous karma.
Without causing any more suffering,
eliminate your own faults. 71

Do what benefits others
without expecting anything in return.
Endure your suffering alone,

and share your pleasures with beggars. 72

Even should you have the perfection of a god,
do not become inflated with pride.
Like a hungry ghost, do not be discouraged
by the hardships of poverty. 73

For your own sake always state a truth
that would even lead to your death
or the loss of your sovereignty.
Never speak in any other fashion. 74

Devote yourself always to the discipline
of acting in accord with your statements.
Glorious one, by that you will become
supremely authoritative for the world. 75

In all cases you should act
after first thoroughly examining (the situation).
By correctly seeing things as they are,
do not become dependent on others. 76

Through the Dharma your kingdom will be happy,
the vast canopy of your fame
will spread in all directions,
and ministers will bow to you. 77

The causes of death are numerous;
those that sustain life are few,
and even they can cause death.
Therefore, always practice the Dharma. 78

If in this way you always practice Dharma,

the contentment that will arise
in you and in the world
will be abundant. 79

Through the Dharma, you will fall asleep easily
and also awake with happy ease.
Since you have no inner problems,
you will also have pleasant dreams. 80

Earnestly serve your parents,
and respect the head of your clan;
enjoy the right things, and be patient and generous;
speak gently without divisiveness,
and practice the discipline of truth.
By doing these in this one life, you will become
king of the gods, and be a godly king even now.
Therefore, devote yourself always to this kind of Dharma. 81–82

Giving the food of three hundred stew-pots[60]
every day, three times a day,
cannot compare to even part of the merit
of just a short moment of love. 83

Even if not liberated, you will attain
these eight excellent qualities from practicing love:
gods and humans will love you,
and they will also protect you;
you will have peace of mind and much happiness
and not be harmed by either poison or weapons;
you will effortlessly attain your aims
and be reborn in the realm of Brahmā. 84–85

If you lead others to develop

bodhicitta, and then make it firm,
you will always have *bodhicitta,*
as stable as the king of mountains itself. 86

Through faith you do not take rebirths that lack freedom.
Through morality, you have positive rebirths.
Through developing (your understanding) of emptiness,
you attain nonattachment to all things. 87

By not being deceptive, you become mindful.
Through reflection, you attain intelligence.
Through reverence, you will realize (the Dharma's) meaning.
Through protecting the Dharma, you will become wise. 88

Through eliminating obscurations
in listening to and imparting the Dharma,
you will gain the companionship of buddhas
and quickly fulfill your desires. 89

Through nonattachment, you accomplish your aims.
Through lack of greed, your possessions increase. Through lack of pride,
you will become prominent. Through tolerance for the Dharma
(of emptiness), you attain the *dhāraṇī* (of not forgetting). 90

Through giving the five quintessentials[61]
and fearlessness to those in fear,
you will become impervious to all demons
and the best of powerful beings. 91

Through giving garlands of lamps to *stūpas,*
lights for those (hindered by) the dark,
and oil for all these lamps,

you will attain the divine eye. 92

By offering cymbals[62] and bells
for the worship of *stūpas*
and also giving conch-horns and drums,
you will attain the divine ear. 93

Do not speak of others' errors
nor mention their physical handicaps.
By carefully protecting their minds,
you will attain the knowledge of others' minds. 94

By providing shoes and conveyances,
attending to those who are weak,
and assisting one's gurus with transportation,
the wise person attains miraculous powers. 95

Through (making efforts) for the sake of the Dharma,
through keeping the Dharma treatises and their meaning in mind,
and through giving the Dharma immaculately,
you will come to remember your past lives. 96

Through correctly and truly understanding
that all things are essenceless,
you will attain the sixth psychic power (*abhijña*)—
the supreme cessation of all defilement. 97

By meditating so as to liberate all beings
upon the uniform awareness of suchness
that has been moistened by compassion,
you will become a Victor with supreme qualities. 98

Due to your various aspirational prayers,

your buddha-field will be pure.
By having offered precious gems to the King of Sages,
you will shine with infinite light. 99

Thus, realize that a karmic effect
corresponds to its karmic cause;
therefore,[63] you should always benefit beings—
this will likewise benefit you. 100

Chapter Four

Royal Policy

If a king acts in a way that contradicts Dharma
or does something that does not make sense,
most of his subjects still praise him; hence,
it is hard for him to know what is appropriate and what is not.[64] 1

If it is even difficult to say something
beneficial but unpleasant to others,
how can I, a monk, hope to do so
to you, the king of a large realm? 2

But because of my affection for you,[65]
and also due to my compassion for beings,
I myself tell you what is
quite helpful, but not very pleasant. 3

The Blessed One said that at the right time
one should say what is true, gentle,
meaningful, and useful to one's disciples out of love.
Hence, I tell you these things. 4

If you remain steadfast[66] while you listen
to a true statement that is not (spoken out of) anger,
then you will accept what you should hear
as if it were pure water that cleanses you. 5

Realizing that what I tell you

is helpful in this context and in others,[67]
implement it for your own sake
and also for the sake of the world. 6

If you do not give away to supplicants
the wealth you obtained through previous giving,[68]
then due to your greed and lack of gratitude,
you will not obtain that wealth again. 7

In this life, a hireling will not bear
your provisions without his wages.
But a lowly beggar, though not paid wages, bears
a hundredfold good qualities to (your) future life. 8

Always keep your mind sublime
and delight in sublime deeds.
All sublime effects
come from sublime actions. 9

Establish glorious Dharma-sites
and famed centers of the three jewels
that have not even been
imagined by weaker kings.[69] 10

You should not make a Dharma-site
that does not give a thrill[70]
to an opulent king, because even
after you die, it will not be praised. 11

With all your resources you should make
those that, for being so exalted,
humble and encourage exalted (kings)
and overwhelm inferior ones. 12

Giving up all of your possessions,
you must go helplessly to some next life,
but before you will go
all that you used for the Dharma. 13

All of a previous king's possessions
come under the control of his successor,[71]
so for that previous king what use will they be
for Dharma, happiness or fame? 14

You get pleasure in this life from enjoying your wealth.
Pleasure in the next life comes from giving it away.
What you have wasted by neither enjoying nor giving
will lead only to suffering—how could it bring happiness?[72] 15

When dying, since you will lose your independence,
you will be unable to give away (your possessions)
through ministers who shamelessly cease to value you
and seek the affection of the new king.[73] 16

Therefore, while healthy, quickly use
all your resources to build Dharma-sites,
for you stand in the midst of death's causes
like a lamp in the midst of a storm. 17

You should also preserve in the manner
in which they have been established
any other Dharma-centers, temples and such
initiated by previous kings. 18

They should be attended by those who practice nonviolence,
who are virtuous in conduct and keep their vows,
who are kind to guests, truthful, and tolerant,[74]

who are not quarrelsome, and are always energetic. 19

The blind, sick and downtrodden,
the homeless, impoverished and crippled
should all, without trouble, equally
obtain food and drink (in those places). 20

Support in an appropriate manner
those Dharma-practitioners who do not seek (aid),
and even support those that are living
in the kingdoms of others. 21

For every Dharma-site appoint officials
of the Dharma who are energetic,
free of greed, knowledgeable, pious,
and who will not hinder those (practicing there). 22

Appoint as ministers policy experts
who are pious, polite, and pure,
devoted, courageous, of good family,
ethically outstanding, and grateful. 23

Appoint military advisors that are generous,
unattached, heroic, and polite,
who properly use (resources),[75] are steadfast,
always vigilant, and pious. 24

Appoint as officials elders that behave
in accord with Dharma and are pure,
who are skillful and know what to do,
who are erudite, organized, impartial and polite. 25

Each month listen to their reports

of all income and expenses;
having listened, tell them all that should be done
for the Dharma-sites and so on. 26

If you rule for the sake of Dharma,
and not for fame or out of desire,
then it will have a most meaningful result—
otherwise, your rule will be disastrous.[76] 27

King, hear how in this world,
where the one usually destroys the other,
you can still have both
the Dharma and a kingdom. 28

May you always be accompanied by many (advisors)
who are mature in knowledge, of good family, well versed
in public policy, afraid of sinning, not contentious
and able to see what should be done. 29

Even if they rightly fine, imprison
or corporally punish (wrongdoers),
you, being always moistened by compassion,
should show kindness (to those punished). 30

King, out of compassion you should always
make your mind focused upon
benefiting all beings, even those
that have committed the most serious sins. 31

You should particularly have compassion for
those that have committed the serious sin
of murder; these ones who have ruined themselves
are indeed worthy of great persons' compassion. 32

Either every day or every five days
release the weakest prisoners.
And see that it is not the case that the remaining ones
are never released, as is appropriate. 33

From thinking that some should never be released
you develop (behaviors and attitudes) that contradict your vows.
From contradicting your vows, you continually
accumulate more negativity. 34

And until they are released,
those prisoners should be made content
by providing them with barbers, baths,
food, drink, and medical care.[77] 35

As if you had the intention of making
unruly children behave properly,
you should discipline them out of compassion—
not out of anger or the desire for material gain. 36

Having properly examined and identified
particularly hateful murderers,
you should send them into exile
without killing or harming them. 37

Independently[78] survey all lands
with your espionage service;
always vigilant and mindful, do
what should be done in accord with Dharma. 38

Through extensive and suitable generosity,
respect and service, devote yourself always
to those who partake of good qualities.

Do the same for the rest, as is appropriate. 39

If the tree of your kingship offers
the shade of tolerance, the open flowers of respect,
and the great fruit of generosity,
then the birds, your subjects, will flock to it. 40

A munificent but majestic king
will be beloved like a sugar-candy
with a hard crust made from
cardamom and black pepper. 41

From reigning properly in this way,[79]
your kingdom will not be chaotic.[80]
It will not proceed improperly, nor contradict
the Dharma. It will be in harmony with the Dharma. 42

You have not brought your kingdom with you
from the previous life, nor will you bring it
to the next. You obtained it through Dharma,
so it is not right to violate Dharma for its sake. 43

King, through your efforts see to it
that you do not end up perpetuating
the stockpiling of suffering
through your kingship's stockpiles. 44

King, through your efforts see to it
that you manage to perpetuate
your stockpile of kingship
through your kingship's stockpiles. 45

Even after a wheel-turning monarch attains

(kingship over) the whole world with its four continents,
pleasure for him is still considered to be
only twofold: physical and mental. 46

A pleasurable physical sensation
is just comparatively less pain.
Mental pleasure—by nature an attitude—
is just conceptually created. 47

Since it is just comparatively less pain
or merely conceptually created,
all the pleasure in the world
is ultimately not really (pleasure). 48

The continents, a country, a place,[81] a house,
a swing,[82] a seat, clothing, a bed,
food, drink, an elephant, a horse, and a woman
are all enjoyed at distinct (points in time). 49

One has "pleasure" through
whichever of these the mind attends to,
but one does not attend to the rest.
Hence, they are not ultimately (causes of pleasure). 50

The five sense faculties such as the eye
do not conceptualize the five kinds of objects
that they apprehend. Therefore, at that time,
one does not (perceive) them as pleasant.[83] 51

When one is aware of one (of the five kinds of) objects
by means of one of the senses, one has no awareness
of the remaining (kinds of objects) by means of the
remaining senses, because (those remaining objects)

are not (taken as) objects at that time. 52

The mind perceives the image of an object
that was perceived in the past by the sense faculties.
Perceiving it, the mind conceptualizes the image
and believes it to be "pleasant." 53

A single sense faculty knows a single (kind of) object.
But without that (object), it is not really (a sense faculty),
and without that (sense faculty),
the object is not really an object. 54

Just as a child comes into existence
in dependence upon its parents,
so too, awareness is said to arise in dependence
upon the eye and a visible form. 55

Past and future objects are unreal, and so are
past and future faculties. (Present ones)
are not distinct from these two (past and future ones).
Hence, the present ones are also unreal. 56

The eye erroneously apprehends the circle
formed by a torch being whirled around.
Likewise, the sense faculties apprehend
objects as if they were in the present. 57

The sense faculties and the sense objects
are thought to be composed of the five elements.
But since each of the elements is unreal,
they also are ultimately unreal. 58

If the elements were distinct from each other, then fire

could occur without fuel. But if they (form a single) composite,
then they have no (distinct) defining characteristics.
This analysis applies to the remaining (four elements). 59

In both these ways the elements are unreal,
so a composite (formed from them) is also unreal.
And since a composite is unreal,
form is also ultimately unreal. 60

Consciousness, sensation, recognition,
and conditioning factors individually
in no way have any ultimate essence.
Therefore, they are ultimately unreal. 61

What one presumes is pleasure
is actually a reduction of pain;
likewise, the suppression of pleasure
is what one presumes to be pain. 62

Since they are essenceless, one eliminates
the craving to obtain pleasure
and the craving to avoid pain.
Those who see them thus[84] attain liberation thereby. 63

"But who does this seeing?"[85] Conventionally, the mind is said
to do so. But without mental functions, there is no mind.
Since (the mind) is unreal,[86] we do not accept that
(two moments of mind) can be simultaneous. 64

Having properly realized that in this way beings
are actually unreal, having no basis (for rebirth),
nor any appropriation (of new aggregates), one attains nirvāṇa
like a fire whose causes have ceased.[87] 65

A bodhisattva, having also had this realization,
becomes firmly intent upon awakening.
It is just due to their compassion that they
continue to take rebirths until awakening. 66

The Tathāgatas taught the bodhisattvas'
collections[88] in the Mahāyāna.
But it is derided by those
who are confused and hateful. 67

Those who deride the Mahāyāna
either cannot distinguish good qualities from faults,
or they mistake good qualities for faults,
or else they hate good qualities. 68

What harms others are faults;
what helps them are good qualities;
recognizing this, it is said that those
who deride the Mahayāna hate good qualities. 69

By[89] being unconcerned about one's own aims,
one takes delight uniquely in the aims of others—
this source of all good qualities is (the teaching of) the Mahāyāna.
Hence, one who hates it is tormented[90] (by negative rebirths). 70

Even a faithful person (is tormented) due to misunderstanding it;
someone else who is angry (is tormented) due to his hatred.
If it is said that even the faithful person is tormented,
what about the one who is hateful? 71

Physicians say that poison
may be eliminated with poison.
So how is it contradictory to say that

suffering may eliminate something unhelpful? 72

(The scriptures) maintain, "The mind is the prerequisite
for all dharmas—the mind is the principle factor (in actions)."
So if one does something helpful with the intention to be helpful,
how could it be unhelpful, even if suffering is involved? 73

If one should do something unpleasant that will later be helpful,
then what about doing something for oneself and for others
that is both pleasant and helpful?
This is an ancient principle (*dharma*). 74

If one will later attain great happiness
from forsaking some trifling pleasure now,
then a sensible[91] person, realizing that s/he will gain
great happiness, should abandon that trifling pleasure now. 75

If you cannot bear this,
then healers and such
who prescribe bitter medicine
would disappear, and that makes no sense. 76

The wise see that in some cases
what is (usually) harmful can be helpful.
All treatises propose both
general rules and exceptions. 77

The Mahāyāna says that all activities
should be motivated by compassion,
and that wisdom will make them pure—[92]
what sensible person would deride this? 78

Discouraged by its vastness and profundity,

ignorant persons, due to their confusion,
today deride the Mahāyāna (and thus become)
the foes of themselves and others. 79

The nature of what the Mahāyāna maintains
is giving, ethics, tolerance, heroic effort,
meditation, wisdom and compassion—
how could it contain a wrong statement? 80

Others' aims are achieved through giving and morality;
one's own, through tolerance and heroic effort;
meditation and wisdom lead to liberation—
this summarizes the Mahāyāna teachings. 81

In brief, the teaching of the Buddha includes
what benefits oneself and others, and (the way to attain)
liberation. These topics are contained in the six perfections.
Therefore, they are also the Buddha's words. 82

Those blinded by ignorance cannot tolerate
the Mahāyāna, in which the buddhas taught
the great path, consisting of merit and wisdom,
that leads to awakening. 83

Since (a Victor comes from) good qualities[93] that are
as inconceivable as space, a Victor is said to have
inconceivable good qualities. Hence, one should admit
the greatness of buddhas, as (explained) in the Mahāyāna. 84

Even just the ethics (of the Buddha)
were beyond even Śāriputra's ken.
Why then would one not admit that
the greatness of the buddhas is inconceivable? 85

The non-arisal taught in the Mahāyāna
and the cessation (taught) for other (Buddhists)
are (both) emptiness. Therefore, one should admit
that cessation and non-arisal are ultimately the same. 86

If through reasoning they see (the doctrines of)
emptiness and the buddhas' greatness in this way,
how could wise people not maintain
that the Mahāyāna and the others are the same? 87

What the Tathāgata stated with a (hidden) intention
is not easy to understand. For this reason,
there is said to be one vehicle, and also three.
Therefore, protect yourself by being equanimous. 88

By being equanimous, you do nothing wrong;
but negativity comes from anger—how could virtue?
Hence, those who seek what is good for themselves[94]
should not despise the Mahāyāna. 89

The bodhisattvas' aspirational prayers
are not taught in the Listeners' vehicle,
nor are their practices, nor the dedication (of merit).
How could one become a bodhisattva through that (vehicle)? 90

(In the other vehicles) the buddhas[95] did not state
the blessings for the bodhisattva's awakening.
What source is better than the Victors
for attaining valid knowledge on this topic? 91

The path that is shared with the Listeners includes the blessings[96]
(for the Arhat), the meanings of the Āryas' Truths,
and the factors of awakening. If buddhahood were the result

of that path, how could buddhahood be superior (to Arhatship)? 92

The subject matter of engaging in practices for awakening
is not discussed in the (Hīnayāna) sūtras,
but it is discussed in the Mahāyāna.
Hence, judicious persons should accept (the Mahāyāna). 93

A grammarian will make (some students)
recite even the alphabet.
Likewise, the Buddha taught the Dharma
in accord with his disciples' abilities.[97] 94

The Dharma he taught to some is for the purpose
of stopping negativity. To some,
it is aimed at the practice of virtue. And to some,
he taught one that is based upon duality. 95

He taught to some a Dharma not based on duality.
And to some, he taught a profound Dharma that terrifies
the timid; its essence is wisdom and compassion,
and it is the means to attain awakening. 96

Hence, the wise should cease
to despise the Mahāyāna,
and they should become more faithful
so as to attain true, complete awakening. 97

Through faith in the Mahāyāna
and by the practices stated therein,
one will attain unexcelled awakening
and all kinds of joy along the way. 98

A Dharma—in essence compassion—

consisting of generosity, morality and tolerance,[98]
was taught especially for householders.
You should resolutely internalize it. 99

However, if you are unable to rule in accord with Dharma,
because the world is opposed to Dharma,
then for the sake of Dharma and glory,
it makes sense for you to become a monk. 100

Chapter Five

Practices of a Bodhisattva

Thereupon, as a monk you should first become serious
about your training, focusing on the *Pratimokṣa*,
including the *Vinaya*, and also on becoming learned
and determining the meaning (of what you study).[99] 1

Then, aware of even the smallest faults, you should eliminate
their basic causes, which should be (eliminated).[100]
Assiduously (learn to) recognize them,
widely known to be fifty-seven (in number). 2

Anger is severe mental agitation;
rancor comes from constantly having it;
Dissimulation is hiding one's negativity;
Hostility is an addiction to negativity. 3

Guile is deceptiveness,
Duplicity, crookedness of mind.
Jealousy is irritation at others' good qualities;
To be miserly is to be afraid to give. 4

Shamelessness is to not be ashamed of yourself;
being brazen is not being embarrassed with regard to others.
To be haughty is to be incapable of honoring others.
Fury is a mental disturbance caused by being angry.[101] 5

Being arrogant is being conceited;

To be heedless is to not apply oneself to virtue.
Pride is of seven kinds;
I will (now) explain each of them. 6

Concerning these, the (first) is called 'pride'—
it is where one thinks of oneself as even
inferior to the inferior, equal to the equal,
or greater than or equal to the inferior. 7

It is 'presumptive pride' for one to presume
that one is equal to someone who is better.
If one presumes oneself to be
even better than one's betters,
then this is pride beyond pridefulness,
thinking oneself to be even loftier than the lofty.[102]
It is excessively bad, like developing
sores on top of your boils. 8–9

The five empty (aggregates)[103]
are called "the appropriated."
When one apprehends them as "I,"
this is called the pride of thinking "I am." 10

To presume that one has attained a result
that one has not attained is to have conceited pride.
The wise know that boasting about
one's negative deeds is wrongful pride. 11

Deriding oneself, thinking
"I cannot manage,"[104]
is the pride of inferiority.
Such are the seven forms of pride, in brief. 12

Hypocrisy is to restrain the senses
for the sake of acquisitions and respect.
Flattery is to utter primarily pleasant phrases
for the sake of acquisitions and respect. 13

Implicit begging is praising others' possessions
so that one might obtain them.
Harassment is openly deriding others
in order to acquire something (from them). 14

The desire to acquire things through what has been acquired
is to praise what has already been acquired (through others' charity).
Carping is constantly remarking on
the mistakes that others have made.[105] 15

Stupefaction is the state of being overwhelmed[106]
that comes from not thinking clearly or from illness,
or else it is a lazy person's negative
attachment to his inferior possessions.[107] 16

The attitude of discrimination is an attitude
obscured by attachment, aversion and confusion.
The failure to examine one's mind
is what is called 'inattention.' 17

Not treating gurus in the manner of the Blessed One
is the loss of respectfulness that occurs
due to being lazy about concordant activities—
it is agreed that this (makes one) a negative person.[108] 18

Longing is a lesser mental obstruction
that comes from passionate desire.
Pining comes from lusting for something;

it is an extreme mental obstruction. 19

Greed is a mental state of attachment
brought about by being attached to one's possessions.
The attachment to others' possessions
is called nonsensical greed.[109] 20

Lusting in opposition to Dharma is to approve
of attachment to women who should be avoided.
Negative desire is when one who does not have
good qualities pretends to have good qualities. 21

Great desire is an extreme yearning
that leaves behind the good fortune of contentment.
Lusting for approval[110] means that one thinks,
"I will be known as having good qualities, no matter what." 22

Intolerance means that one is unable to bear it
when (others) do one harm or when one suffers.
Impropriety is the failure to respect what should be done
with regard to preceptors and gurus. 23

Not heeding instructions means that one does not
take seriously statements that accord with Dharma.[111]
Rampant conceptuality concerning one's relatives is
an attachment that (arises through) loving one's relatives. 24

Likewise, to be attached to one's country[112]
is to overstate its good qualities.
And the fanciful notion that one will not die means
that one is not concerned with death due to fearing it. 25

Rampant conceptuality in connection

with recognition is thinking,
"Somehow (I must make) people take me
as their guru by virtue of my excellent qualities." 26

Rampant conceptuality in connection
with infatuation is dwelling on how
one might help or hurt others, due to
being affected by attachment or malice for them. 27

Displeasure is a state of mind fouled
by longing on the part of an irresolute (person).[113]
Lassitude is the laziness of one who lacks energy—
it comes from being physically listless.[114] 28

Disfiguration is the transformation of body and face
that occurs due to negative mental states.
The lack of desire for food[115] is the physical
stupor[116] that comes from eating too much. 29

It is taught that the state of extreme
mental dejection is mental depression.
Longing for the desirable is yearning
for (experiences of) the five sensory objects. 30

Harmful intent comes from nine causes—
it is the intent to harm others on the part of one who is
concerned about some misfortune in the three times
with regard to oneself, one's friends, or one's enemies. 31

Sluggishness is a state of inactivity
due to physical and mental heaviness.
Torpor is sleep; excitement is
a lack of physical and mental tranquillity. 32

Regret is to lament one's negative activities;
it arises from agonizing about them later.
Doubt is to be of two minds about
the (Four Noble) Truths, the Three Jewels, and so on. 33

A bodhisattva should forsake these (faults)—
one with (monastic) vows must forsake even more—
since[117] when one is freed of these faults,
one can easily develop positive qualities. 34

In short, the good qualities that
a bodhisattva should develop
are generosity, morality, tolerance, heroic effort,
concentration, wisdom, loving kindness, and so on. 35

To be generous is to give up one's wealth;
to be moral is to endeavor to help others;
tolerance is the abandonment of anger;
heroic effort is enthusiasm for virtue. 36

Concentration is unafflicted one-pointedness;
wisdom is definitively determining the truths' meaning.
Loving kindness is a state of mind that savors only
compassion for all sentient beings. 37

From generosity comes wealth, happiness from morality.
From tolerance comes beauty, splendor from heroic effort.
Through meditation, one is peaceful, through understanding
comes liberation. Compassion is what accomplishes all aims. 38

Through the simultaneous
perfection of all these seven,
one attains the object of inconceivable wisdom—

lordship over the world. 39

Just as eight stages of the Listener
are discussed in the Listener's Vehicle,
so too, the ten stages of the bodhisattva
are taught in the Mahāyāna. 40

The first of these is (called) the Joyous
because the bodhisattva experiences great joy,
since the three entanglements have been eliminated
and s/he has been born into the Tathāgata-family. 41

Through the maturation of that (stage),
the perfection of generosity becomes supreme,
s/he is able to make a hundred worlds quake,
and s/he becomes the Great Lord of Jambudvīpa. 42

The second stage is called the Immaculate
because (the bodhisattva's) tenfold activities
of body, speech and mind are immaculate,
and s/he naturally adheres to those (moral activities). 43

Through the maturation of that (stage)
the perfection of morality becomes supreme,
s/he becomes a glorious ruler with the seven treasures,
a wheel-turning monarch, beneficent to beings. 44

Through its maturation, s/he becomes
a monarch that rules all four continents,
and s/he gains expertise in
turning beings away from immorality.[118] 44a

The third stage is (called) the Radiant

because the light of peaceful wisdom arises,
the concentrations and psychic powers have arisen,
and attachment and anger have completely ceased. 45

Through the maturation of that (stage),
s/he practices supreme tolerance and heroic effort;
s/he becomes the celestials' skilled, great Lord
who averts all sensual desire. 46

The fourth (stage) is called the Brilliant
because the brilliance of true wisdom arises,
and (the bodhisattva) distinctively develops
all the factors of awakening. 47

Through the maturation of that (stage), s/he becomes
the celestial ruler in the abode of the Suyāma (deities).
S/he becomes skilled, destroying the source
of the belief that the transitory aggregates (are the Self).[119] 48

The fifth is the Indomitable, since one
cannot be subdued by any demon,
and one gains expertise in knowing
the subtle meaning of the Ārya's Truths and such. 49

Through the maturation of that (stage)
s/he becomes the celestial ruler of Tuṣita
and refutes all the Tīrthikas' beliefs
concerning (the efficacy) of austerities.[120] 50

The sixth is called the Approaching because
s/he approaches the qualities of a buddha
and is enhanced by the attainment of cessation
through inculcating insight and quiescence. 51

Through the maturation of that (stage), s/he becomes
lord of the celestials who delight in emanations.[121]
Unsurpassable by the listeners,
s/he eliminates arrogant pride. 52

The seventh is the Far Advanced because
the number (of excellent qualities) has advanced far,
since on this (stage) s/he enters moment by moment
into the state of meditative cessation. 53

Through the maturation of that (stage),
s/he becomes the powerful ruler of the celestials.[122]
S/he becomes a great leader of Jñānācāryas,
knowing the realizations of the Āryas' Truths. 54

The eighth is the youth's stage, the Immovable,
because, free of concepts, s/he is unshakable.
The range of his physical, vocal,
and mental activity is inconceivable. 55

Through the maturation of that (stage),
s/he becomes a Brahmā who rules a kilocosm;
s/he is unsurpassed by the Listeners and Solitary Buddhas
in determining the meaning (of the Dharma). 56

The ninth, like a regency,
is called the Genius, since by
attaining true awareness, (the bodhisattva)
has excellent understanding on this (stage). 57

Through the maturation of this (stage),
s/he becomes the lord of a bikilocosm;
s/he is unsurpassed by the Arhats and such

regarding qualms in the minds of beings. 58

The tenth is the Dharma Cloud because
the (bodhisattva) rains down the holy Dharma,
and the bodhisattva is anointed
with rays of light by the buddhas. 59

Through the maturation of that (stage),
s/he becomes the celestial ruler of the Pure Realm,
master of inconceivable wisdom's object,
supreme among great lords. 60

These ten are renowned as
the ten bodhisattva stages.
The buddhas' stage is different—
in all ways immeasurably vast.
It is merely called,
"Possessing Ten Powers."
Each of those powers is as limitless
as (the infinite number of) beings. 61–62

For the buddhas are merely said
to be inestimable, just as the space,
earth, water and wind
of all regions is also limitless. 63

If one does not see that their causes
cannot be measured to some fixed extent,
then one will not be confident
that the buddhas are inestimable. 64

Therefore, each day, three times a day,
before an icon, *stūpa*, or elsewhere,

you should perform the recitation
of the following twenty verses: 65

[*Here begins the Twenty Verse Prayer*]

Honoring in all ways the buddhas,
the Dharma, the community, and also
the bodhisattvas, to them I go for refuge,
and pay homage to those worthy of homage. 66

I turn away from all negativity
and embrace all (kinds of) merit;
I rejoice in all the merit
(amassed by) all sentient beings. 67

With bowed head and palms together
I beseech all perfect buddhas
to turn the wheel of Dharma, and
remain as long as beings remain. 68

Through the merit of doing this and
the merit I have done and not yet done,
may all sentient beings be endowed
with unsurpassed *bodhicitta.* 69

May all sentient beings have immaculate
faculties and transcend the unfree (states);
may they control their own actions
and live by a good livelihood. 70

May all embodied beings have jewels
in their hands, and may a limitless (amount)
of all kinds of necessities remain

inexhaustible for as long as *saṃsāra* endures. 71

At all times may all women
become supreme persons.[123]
May all beings be endowed
with intelligence and legs.[124] 72

May all beings have a good complexion
and also a good physique. May they be radiant
and pleasant to behold. Free of illness,
may they be strong and live long. 73

May they all gain expertise in the methods,
and become free of all suffering.
May they become devoted to the Three Jewels
and have the great treasure of Buddha Dharma. 74

May they be adorned with love, compassion, joy,
(the ability to) remain equanimous in the face of hardship,[125]
generosity, morality, patience, heroic effort,
meditative concentration and wisdom. 75

Thus adorned, may they complete all the collections,
and (obtaining) brilliant marks and secondary signs,
may they traverse without hindrance
the ten stages (to) the inconceivable. 76

May I also become adorned with
these good qualities and all others as well;
may I become freed from all faults,
and may I attain supreme love for all beings;[126]
may I perfect the virtues
to which all beings aspire,

and may I always dispel the suffering
of all embodied beings. 77–78

In all worlds may all beings
who are feeling anxious due to fear
become completely fearless
merely by hearing my name. 79

From seeing and thinking[127] of me,
and from merely hearing my name,
may beings become clear-minded,
undisturbed and at ease;[128]
may it be definite that they will awaken,
and in all their future lives,
may they attain the five psychic powers.
In all ways may I always do what brings
benefit and happiness to all beings. 80–81

May I always dissuade all at once
all those beings of any world
who intend to engage in negativity
without doing them any harm. 82

Like the earth, water, wind, and fire,
medicinal herbs, and the trees of the wilderness,
may I always be made use of freely
by all beings just as they wish. 83

May I be beloved of beings, and may they
be more beloved to me than myself.
May I bear the results of their negativity,
and may they have the results of all my virtue. 84

As long as there is even some single[129]
sentient being somewhere who is not yet free,
may I remain (in the world) for that being's sake,
even if I have attained unexcelled awakening. 85

[*Here ends the Twenty Verse Prayer*]

If the merit of making such statements
were to be a material thing,
it would not fit into worlds
as numerous as the sands of the Ganges. 86

This is what the Blessed One said,
and the reason is here to be seen—
the worlds of beings are infinite,
and the intention to aid them is likewise. 87

Thus ends[130] my brief explanation
of the Dharma to you. Always consider
this Dharma to be beloved to you, just as
you are beloved to yourself.[131] 88

One who considers the Dharma to be beloved
is truly holding himself as beloved.
For if one wants to benefit those whom one loves,
one can do so by means of the Dharma. 89

Therefore, be devoted to Dharma, just as you are devoted to yourself.
Be devoted to realization, just as you are devoted to Dharma.
Be devoted to wisdom, just as you are devoted to realization.
Be devoted to the wise, just as you are devoted to wisdom. 90

One who, due to his own failings, has doubts

about a pure, loving and intelligent (teacher)
who speaks with restraint about what is helpful
is ruining his (chances of attaining) his aims.[132] 91

Thinking, "I am under the care of one
who is pure, loving, and wise
and who states with restraint what is helpful,"
vow to spiritually discipline yourself, king.[133] 91a

Know, in brief, the qualifications
of spiritual friends. You should receive
teachings from those who are content,
compassionate and moral, and possess
the wisdom that dispels negative mental states.
Having understood (what they teach), you should
respectfully put it into practice. Through this excellent
system, you will attain the supreme achievement. 92–93

Speak the truth, and speak gently to beings.
Be pleasant, unassailable and skilled in public
policy;[134] do not wish to humiliate others;
be independent, and always speak well. 94

With enmity well subdued,[135] be generous,
dignified, and mentally peaceful. Do not
procrastinate, and do not be rash;
do not be dishonest, and be courteous.[136] 95

Be auspicious[137] like the full moon,
and radiant like the autumn sun.
Be profound like the ocean,
and steadfast, like Mount Meru. 96

Freed from all negativities
and adorned with all good qualities,
be the sustenance of all beings,
and become omniscient. 97

This Dharma is not explained
only for a king. It is also taught,
as is appropriate, to other beings
out of the desire to benefit them. 98

King, it would be good for you
to contemplate[138] this discourse every day,
so that you and other beings
might attain true, complete awakening. 99

Be moral, and have the highest[139] respect for gurus;
be patient, devoid of jealousy and greed.
(Enjoy) the wealth of aiding others without expectation of return,
and be helpful to those who are deprived.
Be devoted to the supreme, avoid those who are not,
and embrace the Dharma.
For the sake of awakening, this is
what those who seek it should always do.[140] 100

[Thus ends the *Precious Garland: An Epistle to a King* by the great master, the Ārya Nāgārjuna. It was originally composed in Sanskrit and then translated into Tibetan by the Indian Master Jñānagarbha and the Tibetan Lotsawa Lui Gyeltsen. The Tibetan translation was then edited and corrected by the Indian Master Kanakavarman and the Tibetan Lotsawa Patsub Nyima Drak. A Sanskrit edition was compiled by Giuseppe Tucci and a corrected edition was prepared by Michael Hahn. Geshe Ngawang Samten compiled a Tibetan edition by collating all the Tibetan versions and comparing them against the Sanskrit. Portions were translated into English by Tucci, and the entire text was translated into English by Jeffrey Hopkins, Anne Klein and Lati Rinpoche. The present translation was made by the Upāsakas John Dunne and Sara McClintock by comparing the Sanskrit editions with the Tibetan prepared by Geshe Samten; the commentaries of the Indian Master Ajitamitra and the Tibetan Scholar-adept Gyaltsab Darma Rinchen were also consulted, as were previous translations. *Sarvaṃ maṅgalam bhavatu*].

The Light of Centrism

In Praise of
the Glorious Protector Nāgārjuna

Könchog Tenpey Drönmey

༄༅། །དཔལ་མགོན་ཀླུ་སྒྲུབ་ཞབས་ལ་བསྟོད་པ་
དབུ་མའི་སྣང་བ་ཞེས་བྱ་བ་བཞུགས་སོ།།

རྒྱལ་བས་ཆོས་ཚུལ་གང་བསྟན་པ།
འགྲོ་བ་མུན་པས་ཁེབས་པ་ལ།
འོད་གསལ་བ་ཡི་ཕྱིར་ཡིན་པས།
སྒྲོན་མ་ཀླུ་སྒྲུབ་རྒྱལ་གྱུར་ཅིག ༡

དམིགས་ལས་དམིགས་པ་རྣམ་མང་བས།།
འགྲོ་བ་དུབ་པར་གྱུར་པ་རྣམས།
དམིགས་པ་མེད་པ་ཞི་བའི་བདེར།
འཁྲིད་པ་ཁྱོད་ནི་དེད་དཔོན་ལགས། ༢

ཤེས་རབ་ཕར་ཕྱིན་ཤེས་རབ་བསླབ།
ཤེས་རབ་མདོ་སྡེའི་མཆོག་གྱུར་ཕྱིར།
ཤེས་རབ་གཞུང་མཆོག་མཛད་པ་ཁྱོད།
བསྟན་འཛིན་ཀུན་ལས་བླ་མར་གྱུར། ༣

རིག་གནས་ཤེས་བྱར་སྤྱོད་ཀུན་ལ།
མུན་སངས་བློ་གྲོས་རབ་རྒྱས་པས།
སངས་རྒྱས་གཉིས་པ་ཀླུ་སྒྲུབ་ཅེས།
དངོས་པོར་སྨྲ་བ་རྣམས་ཀྱང་འདུད། ༤

The Light of Centrism:

In Praise of the Glorious Protector Nāgārjuna

[At the start of each day of the teachings on the *Precious Garland* to be given by His Holiness the XIVth Dalai Lama in Los Angeles in June, 1997, His Holiness will recite this praise to Nāgārjuna in Tibetan. He will then recite verses 5.66–5.85 of the *Precious Garland* itself, the translation of which can be found earlier in this book.]

The Dharma that the Victor taught
is for the sake of shining light upon
beings enveloped in the darkness (of ignorance):
hence, victory to the lamp, Nāgārjuna! 1

Beings are exhausted by the proliferation
of perceptions through perceiving. You lead
them to the bliss of peace, the imperceptible;
as such, you are the great Guide. 2

The perfection of wisdom and the higher training in wisdom
are the supreme aspects of the wisdom *sūtras.*
Hence, you composed the supreme wisdom treatises—
among all teaching-holders, you are the guru. 3

Your intellect became fully expanded (*rgyas*), eliminating (*sangs*)
dark confusion about all sciences and all that can be known;
hence, you are called "Nāgārjuna, the second Buddha (*sangs rgyas*)."
Even the Essentialists bow down to you. 4

མ་རིག་འགག་པས་ཡན་ལག་ཀུན།
འགག་པར་མདོ་སྡེ་ཀུན་གསུངས་ཀྱང་།
གབ་པ་སྲིད་པའི་སྲོག་རྩ་ནི།
གསལ་བར་གཅོད་པའི་རིགས་པ་བྱིན། ༥

གཞན་དག་སྟོང་ཞེས་བཀག་པ་དང་།
བརྟེན་ཞེས་སྒྲུབ་པ་ཉིད་གོ་བས།
ཐག་མཁན་སྣབས་བཞིན་ཕྱོགས་སུ་ལྷུང་།
ཁྱོད་ཀྱིས་བཟློག་སླེ་བདེ་བར་བཞུགས། ༦

རྒྱ་རྐྱེན་ཡན་ལག་དུ་མ་ཞིག
ཚོགས་ནས་ཕར་ལ་འཇོག་དགོས་པ།
ཚུགས་ཐུབ་རང་དབང་བྲལ་བའི་རྟགས།
དེས་ནི་རྟེན་འབྱུང་སྟོང་པར་བཤད། ༧

རང་དབང་ངོ་བོ་མ་དམིགས་ཀྱང་།
སྣ་ཚོགས་སྣང་བ་མི་འགོག་པས།
རྐྱེན་ཚོགས་འཛའ་མཚོན་སྣང་ཙམ་དང་།
འདྲ་བར་སྟོང་པས་རྟེན་འབྱུང་གསུངས། ༨

Although all *sūtras* say that by stopping ignorance,
all factors (of existence in saṃsāra) are stopped,
it is obscure, but you (clarified and) bestowed the reasoning
that clearly cuts the vitals of saṃsāra. 5

Others understand "emptiness" to mean the refutation (of things)
and "dependent" to mean that (things are) established. Thus,
like one weaving (separate threads), they fall into an (extreme) position.
But doing the opposite, you easily remain (without falling into extremes). 6

(Anything that arises from) a collection of causes and conditions,
or is a collection of many parts, is necessarily oppositionally posited.
Its lack of independence and autonomy is the evidence
due to which you said that the interdependent is (necessarily) empty. 7

Although one cannot perceive any autonomous essence, the appearance
of the variegated (world) is not negated. Therefore, you said that,
like a rainbow which merely appears, (anything that is) causally conditioned
or a collection (of parts) is interdependently arisen, because it is empty. 8

མ་ཚོགས་པ་ལ་གནས་མེད་ཅིང་།
བརྒྱ་སྟོང་ཚོགས་ལ་གཅིག་པ་མེད།
གཅིག་མེད་པ་ལ་དུ་མ་མེད།
གཅིག་དང་གཞན་མིན་ཅི་ཡང་མེད། ༩

དངོས་པོ་རྫས་དང་ལྡོག་པ་ལས།
གཅིག་དང་ཐ་དད་རྣམ་འབྱེད་པ།
གཉིས་ལ་ལྟེ་གཉིས་སླ་བའི་ཚིག
ཇི་བཞིན་བདེན་པར་ག་ལ་འགྱུར། ༡༠

དེ་བཞིན་ལ་ལར་སྐྱེ་དང་ཡོད།
གཞན་འགར་འགག་དང་མེད་པ་སོགས།
རེས་འགའ་བ་ཀུན་རྫུན་པ་སྟེ།
བདེན་པ་གཅིག་ལས་འགྱུར་བ་མེད། ༡༡

ཡོད་ན་རྟག་ཏུ་ཡོད་པ་ལ།
རྒྱུན་གྱིས་ཅི་བྱ་གཉིས་ཀ་མཉམ།
མེད་པར་བདེན་པ་འབྱུང་མི་སྲིད།
ཤི་བ་པོས་ཀྱང་མགྲོན་དུ་མིན། ༡༣

There is no abiding in that which is not a collection,
and no singularity in a collection of a hundred thousand (parts).
Without singularity there is no plurality.
And there is nothing that is neither singular nor plural. 9

One might analyze a thing as being both singular and plural
in terms of its substantiality and its exclusions;
But this is speaking of duality with a forked tongue; how could
the words of one who speaks this way be true just as they are? 10

Likewise, in some cases, (it is said that things) are produced and exist,
and in some cases, (it is said that things) have ceased and do not exist.
These contingent (claims) are all false.
From being just real, there would be no change.[141] 11

If something were (truly) existent, then it would always exist.
What would causal conditions do? Both are the same.
In the case of the nonexistent, it is impossible
for the real to occur. The dead cannot be guests. 12

རྒྱུ་ལ་རྒྱུ་ཡི་དངོས་གནས་ཆེ།
འབྲས་བུར་དེ་འཆར་སྨྱུག་བཞིན་ན།
སྐྱོང་ཕྱིར་སྐྱོང་ཙམ་དེར་འཆར་དེ།
མཁའ་ཉིད་སྣང་དང་མུན་པ་བཞིན། ༧༣

ཐ་དད་སྐྱོས་མེད་རྒྱུ་འབྲས་མིན།
ཡང་ན་ཀུན་ཀྱང་དེར་བརྗོད་རུང་།
ཐེར་ཟུག་རྒྱུ་ནི་འབྲས་བུའི་གེགས།
དེ་ཡིས་གྲོལ་བའི་སྐབས་ཀྱང་ཅི། ༧༤

དབང་བསྒྱུར་བདེན་པ་བཅོས་མེད་ལ།
བདེན་མིན་བཅིངས་ཀྱང་ཐབས་གཞན་ལྡན།
གྲོལ་སོགས་རུང་བཞིས་བདེན་གཉིས་ཀྱི།
སྒྲུབ་པས་ཐར་འདོད་དབུགས་དབྱུངས་མཛད། ༧༥

ལྷ་ངན་ཀུན་གཙོ་འཇིག་ཚོགས་ལ།
ལྷ་བ་སྲིད་པའི་རྩ་བ་ནི།
ལྷ་ཀུན་མཆོག་གྱུར་མཐའ་བྲལ་གྱི།
ལྷ་བས་བཅད་ཉིད་ཐར་པར་བཞེད། ༧༦

If, when the cause actually abides as a cause,
it arises as an effect, like a sprout, then since
it is empty, it arises as what is merely empty,
like light and darkness in the sky. 13

(Things that) are distinct and non-dependent cannot be
cause and effect; otherwise, one could say that everything is.
An unchanging cause prevents any effect—
what chance would there be of becoming free thereby? 14

Being under the control of what is truly real is irreparable;
but if (beings) are bound (by) the unreal, there are other methods.
Accepting that liberation and such is thus possible, you established
the two truths and thereby relieved those who seek liberation. 15

Among all negative views, the chief one is the belief
that the transitory aggregates (are the self);
it is saṃsāra's root. You affirm that it is cut by the best of all views,
the view free of extremes, and that one is thus liberated. 16

དེ་ཕྱིར་བགྲོད་གཅིག་ཤེས་རབ་རྨད།
འོན་ཀྱང་ཐེག་ཆེན་ནམ་མཁའ་ལྟར།
བྱེད་པོ་ཐབས་ཉེ་དེ་བས་རྨད།
དེས་ན་ཟབ་རྒྱས་ཟུང་དུ་མཛོད། ༢༧

སྟོང་ཡང་སྙིང་ངོ་ཞེས་བྱ་འདིས།
བདེན་པའི་བྱ་བྱེད་རང་རོང་གི
འགལ་འདུའི་མི་བདེ་ཀུན་བསྐྱལ་བས།
ཀླན་ཀའི་གོ་སྐབས་ཡོངས་ལས་འདས། ༢༨

ཡོད་མེད་མཐའ་བྲལ་དབུ་མའི་ལམ།
ཡོད་མེད་མཐའ་སྤངས་ཟུང་འཇུག་དོན།
གསལ་བར་ལུང་བསྟན་གསལ་བ་གཉིས།
རྒྱལ་བའི་དགོངས་པ་ཚད་མར་གནས། ༢༩

མར་མེ་མཛད་ཀྱང་བྱོན་པའི་སྔར།
ལུང་བསྟན་བརྙེས་པས་དཔག་དཀའ་ཡང་།
ཕལ་པ་ལྟ་བུར་བྱིན་རློབས་པ།
རྒྱལ་བའི་རྣམ་འཕྲུལ་བསམ་མི་ཁྱབ། ༣༠

Hence, wisdom, the one way (to freedom)
is wondrous, but the Mahāyāna's
space-like agent, method, is even more amazing.
Therefore, integrate the profound and the expansive. 17

The (understanding), "It is empty, yet appearing,"
smoothes out all unease about contradictions
concerning the uneven (ground of) real functionality;
hence, one transcends any possibility of objection. 18

The two clarifiers who had been clearly foretold
clarified that the middle way, free of extremes, means
the integration that forsakes all essentialism and nihilism—
those two are authorities on the Victor's intention. 19

Even before the coming of Dīpaṃkara, he received
the prediction (of awakening); therefore, he is
difficult to fathom, and yet he was blessed like an ordinary being—
the miraculous emanations of the Victor are inconceivable! 20

ཟུང་མིན་དོན་མིན་ཀུན་བསལ་ཏེ།
ཆོས་འདུལ་ལྷ་དང་འདུས་པའི་གནད།
གསལ་མཛད་སངས་རྒྱས་གཉིས་པ་དང་།
རྒྱལ་བ་གཉིས་པ་མཚན་དོན་གཅིག ༣༡

དེ་དག་གཤེགས་བཤུལ་ནང་གནས་ཀྱང་།
འཕྲེ་བོ་བདག་ཅག་བགྲོད་ནུས་མིན།
རྗེས་སུ་འོ་དོད་འབོད་པ་བཞིན།
གདུང་བའི་དབྱངས་ཀྱིས་གསོལ་བ་འདེབས། ༣༢

གུས་པས་གསོལ་བཏབ་དགེ་སྨིན་པས།
རྒྱ་ཆེན་ཐབས་ཀྱི་གཤོག་རླབས་ཅན།
ཟབ་མོའི་དེ་ཉིད་རིག་པ་ཡིས།
དོན་གཉིས་མཁའ་ལ་བགྲོད་གྱུར་ཅིག ༣༣

He refuted the impossible and the senseless,
and clarified the essential points of the Dharma,
the Vinaya, the (right) view, and the Guhyasamāja—
the names 'Second Buddha' and 'Second Victor' are the same. 21

Although we live in the tracks they left behind,
we who crawl cannot traverse that path.
But crying out like one left behind,
we make supplication with a pained lament. 22

Through the matured virtue of our respectful supplications,
may we gain the powerful wings of vast method,
and aware of the suchness of the profound,
let us make our way through the sky to our two goals. 23

[At the request of Halha Rabjampa Sangyey, the monk Könchog Tenpey Drönmey (1762-1824) composed this text called, *The Light of Centrism: A Praise to Nāgārjuna.* At the request of Thubten Dhargye Ling, it was translated by the Upāsakas John Dunne and Sara McClintock according to the interpretation of the Venerable Geshe Gyeltsen.]

Twenty Verse Praise from The Precious Garland

Chapter 5, vv. 66-85

སངས་རྒྱས་དམ་ཆོས་དགེ་འདུན་དང་།
བྱང་ཆུབ་སེམས་དཔའ་རྣམས་ལ་ཡང་།
རྣམ་ཀུན་བདུད་དེ་སྐྱབས་མཆིས་ནས།
མཆོད་འོས་རྣམས་ལ་ཕྱག་འཚལ་ལོ།

སྡིག་པ་རྣམས་ལས་ལྡོག་བགྱི་ཞིང་།
བསོད་ནམས་ཐམས་ཅད་ཡོངས་སུ་གཟུང་།
ལུས་ཅན་ཀུན་གྱི་བསོད་ནམས་དག
ཀུན་ལ་རྗེས་སུ་ཡི་རང་ངོ་།

བདག་ནི་སྤྱིས་བཏུད་ཐལ་སྦྱར་ཏེ།
ཆོས་ཀྱི་འཁོར་ལོ་བསྐོར་སླད་དང་།
འགྲོ་གནས་བར་དུ་བཞུགས་སླད་དུ།
རྫོགས་པའི་སངས་རྒྱས་རྣམས་ལ་གསོལ།

དེ་ལྟར་བགྱིས་པའི་བསོད་ནམས་དང་།
བདག་གིས་བགྱིས་དང་མ་བགྱིས་གང་།
དེས་ནི་སེམས་ཅན་ཐམས་ཅད་ཀྱང་།
བླ་མེད་བྱང་ཆུབ་སེམས་ལྡན་ཤོག །

སེམས་ཅན་ཐམས་ཅད་དྲི་མེད་དབང་།
ཡོངས་རྫོགས་མི་ཁོམ་ཀུན་འདས་ཤིང་།
སྤྱོད་པ་རང་དབང་ཡོད་པ་དང་།
འཚོ་བ་བཟང་དང་ལྡན་པར་ཤོག

ལུས་ཅན་དག་ནི་ཐམས་ཅད་ཀྱང་།
ལག་ན་རིན་ཆེན་ཉིད་ལྡན་ཞིང་།
ཡོ་བྱད་ཐམས་ཅད་མཐའ་ཡས་པ།
འཁོར་བ་སྲིད་དུ་མི་ཟད་ཤོག

བུད་མེད་ཐམས་ཅད་དུས་ཀུན་དུ།
སྐྱེས་མཆོག་ཉིད་དུ་འགྱུར་བར་ཤོག
ལུས་ཅན་ཐམས་ཅད་རིག་པ་དང་།
རྐང་པར་ལྡན་པ་ཉིད་དུ་ཤོག

ལུས་ཅན་ཁ་དོག་ལྡན་པ་དང་།
གཟུགས་བཟང་གཟི་བརྗིད་ཆེ་བ་དང་།
བལྟ་ན་སྡུག་ཅིང་ནད་མེད་དང་།
སྟོབས་ཆེན་ཚེ་དང་ལྡན་པར་ཤོག

ཐམས་ཅད་ཐབས་ལ་མཁས་གྱུར་ཏེ། |
སྡུག་བསྔལ་ཀུན་ལས་ཐར་པ་དང་། |
དཀོན་ཅོག་གསུམ་ལ་གཞོལ་བ་དང་། |
སངས་རྒྱས་ཆོས་ནོར་ཆེར་ལྡན་ཤོག |

བྱམས་དང་སྙིང་རྗེ་དགའ་བ་དང་། |
ཉོན་མོངས་བཏང་སྙོམས་གནས་པ་དང་། |
སྦྱིན་དང་ཚུལ་ཁྲིམས་བཟོད་བརྩོན་འགྲུས། |
བསམ་གཏན་ཤེས་རབ་ཀྱིས་བརྒྱན་ཅིང་། |

ཚོགས་རྣམས་ཐམས་ཅད་ཡོངས་རྫོགས་ཏེ། |
མཚན་དང་དཔེ་བྱད་གསལ་བ་དང་། |
བསམ་གྱིས་མི་ཁྱབ་ས་བཅུ་དག |
རྒྱུན་མི་ཆད་པར་བགྲོད་པར་ཤོག |

བདག་ཀྱང་ཡོན་ཏན་དེ་དག་དང་། |
གཞན་ཀུན་ཀྱིས་ཀྱང་རྣམ་བརྒྱན་ཏེ། |
ཉེས་པ་ཀུན་ལས་གྲོལ་བ་དང་། |
སེམས་ཅན་ཀུན་མཆོག་བྱམས་པ་དང་། |

སེམས་ཅན་ཀུན་ཡོད་རེ་བ་ཡི། |
དགེ་བ་ཐམས་ཅད་རྫོགས་བགྱིད་ཅིང་། |
རྟག་ཏུ་ལུས་ཅན་ཐམས་ཅད་ཀྱི། |
སྡུག་བསྔལ་སེལ་བར་བགྱིད་པར་ཤོག |

འཇིག་རྟེན་ཀུན་ལ་སྐྱེ་བོ་གང་། |
སུ་དག་འཇིགས་པས་སྐྲོ་བ་དེ། |
བདག་གི་མིང་ཙམ་ཐོས་པས་ཀྱང་། |
ཤིན་ཏུ་འཇིགས་པ་མེད་པར་ཤོག |

བདག་ནི་མཐོང་དང་དྲན་པ་དང་། |
མིང་ཙམ་ཐོས་པས་སྐྱེ་བོ་རྣམས། |
རབ་དགའ་འཁྲུལ་མེད་རྣལ་མར་དང་། |
རྫོགས་པའི་བྱང་ཆུབ་ངེས་པ་དང་། |

ཚེ་རབས་ཀུན་ཏུ་རྗེས་འབྲང་བའི། |
མངོན་ཤེས་ལྔ་པོ་ཐོབ་པར་ཤོག |
སེམས་ཅན་ཀུན་ལ་རྣམ་ཀུན་ཏུ། |
རྟག་ཏུ་ཕན་བདེ་བགྱིད་པར་ཤོག |

འཇིག་རྟེན་ཀུན་ན་སྐྱེ་བོ་གང་། །
སྡིག་པ་བྱེད་པར་འདོད་འགྱུར་བ། །
དེ་དག་ཐམས་ཅད་གནོད་མེད་པར། །
རྟག་ཏུ་ཅིག་ཙར་བཟློག་གྱུར་ཅིག །

ས་དང་ཆུ་དང་མེད་དང་རླུང་། །
སྨན་དང་དགོན་པའི་ཤིང་བཞིན་དུ། །
རྟག་ཏུ་སེམས་ཅན་ཐམས་ཅད་ཀྱིས། །
རང་དགར་དགག་མེད་སྤྱད་པར་ཤོག །

སེམས་ཅན་རྣམས་ལ་སྲོག་བཞིན་ཕངས། །
བདག་ལས་དེ་དག་ཆེས་ཕངས་ཤོག །
བདག་ལ་དེ་དག་སྡིག་སྨིན་ཅིང་། །
བདག་དགེ་མ་ལུས་དེར་སྨིན་ཤོག །

ཇི་སྲིད་སེམས་ཅན་འགའ་ཞིག་ཀྱང་། །
གང་དུ་མ་གྲོལ་དེ་སྲིད་དུ། །
དེ་ཕྱིར་བླ་ན་མེད་པ་ཡི། །
བྱང་ཆུབ་ཐོབ་ཀྱང་གནས་གྱུར་ཅིག །

Notes

1 Tucci, *Journal of the Royal Asiatic Society* 1935: 307-25; 1936: 237-52 and 423-35. Hopkins, et. al., *The Precious Garland and the Song of the Four Mindfulnesses* (New York: Harper and Row, 1975).

2 Ajitamitra (7) and Gyaltsab-je (5a) comment that the Sanskrit word *dharma* (Tib., *chos*) is derived from a verbal root (*dhṛ*) that has the sense of "to hold" or "to restrain." They note that the Dharma, or spiritual teachings of the Buddha, "holds" or "restrains" one from falling into the abyss of lower rebirths and cyclic existence in general.

3 Tib. reads *gnag lam* for Skt. *godaṇḍaka*, the latter most accurately meaning a "line of cattle." As Ajitamitra (23) and Gyaltsab-je (8b) make clear, the point of this metaphor is that when the leading animal in a herd of cattle sets off, the other animals follow whatever path the leading animal happens to choose, even if that path is the wrong path.

4 Tib. *'khyud pa* carries the sense of "wrapped with" or "entwined." The Sanskrit text, however, reads *avalīḍha*, meaning "ravished" or "gnawed."

5 "Savage snakes" translate Tib. *gdugs pa* (or *gdug pa*) which renders Skt. *vyāla*. This Sanskrit word *vyāla* can serve as either an adjective or a noun. As an adjective, it means "cruel," "savage" and so on. As a noun, it means ferocious animal, leopard, snake, tiger and such. Gyaltsab-je (9a) glosses *gdug pa* as *sbrul gdug pa*, which suggests that he understands *vyāla* to be used as both an adjective and a noun here.

6 "This Dharma" refers here specifically to the "Dharma of elevation," as is made explicit at the end of this section in verse 1.24. In the subsequent section, Nāgārjuna goes on to explain the "Dharma of the highest good."

7 The phrase "appears profoundly" renders Skt. *gambhīradarśana* and Tib. *zab par snang ba*. Gyaltsab-je (11a) comments on the verse as follows: "The

Dharma of the highest good—the cognitive object of the wisdom that realizes essencelessness, namely, the essencelessness of persons and the essencelessness of things—is difficult for other, ordinary beings and for conventional awareness to realize. Hence, it is 'subtle'; and since it is difficult for others to plumb the depths of it, it appears to the wise ones as profound."

8 The five "aggregates" (Skt. *skandha*, Tib. *phungs po*) are the five psychophysical components of the body-mind system. They are form (Skt. *rūpa*), sensation (Skt. *vedanā*), recognition (Skt. *saṃjñā*), mental conditioning (Skt. *saṃskāra*), and consciousness (Skt. *vijñāna*).

9 We translate "monks and nuns" for Skt. *bhikṣu* and Tib. *dge slong* since the masculine term can include the feminine in both languages. In addition, it is well known that Ānanda taught the Dharma to both monks and nuns.

10 The syntax of the Sanskrit suggests a slightly different translation: "Having listened thus to the Dharma that puts an end to suffering, the undiscerning are terrified, (and) since they do not understand, they fear the fearless state."

11 Skt. *priya* is rendered in this line as *'dod*, but in the last line it is translated *dga'*. One might understand *'dod* in this line to mean "asserted," but this would be a strange interpretation of *priya*. Tucci (317) follows the reading we have proposed, although Hopkins (23) understands *'dod* here as "asserted."

12 The verse has been translated according to Gyaltsab-je (15a). However, according to the Sanskrit text and to Ajitamitra (53), the verse should be translated as follows: "Through wisdom, one subdues the (notions of) existence and nonexistence, and one thus transcends sin and merit. Thereby, one transcends high and low rebirths; the holy ones call that liberation."

13 Samten (54) has a long note on this verse, in which he shows that the canonical version of the second line of this verse is almost certainly corrupt. He thus emends the verse as follows: *sngar skyes pa dang lhan cig skyes / rgyu ni don du rgyu min no / btags dang yang dag nyid du na / skye ba'ng rab tu ma grags phyir.* The Sanskrit reads: *prāgjātaḥ sahajātaś ca hetur ahetuko 'rthataḥ / prajnapter apratītatvād utpatteś caiva tattvataḥ.*

We have translated according to Samten's emendation, which agrees with the Sanskrit and Ajitamitra (53-54). If, however, we follow the canonical version and Gyaltsab-je (15b), we get the following translation: "(A cause) that occurs before (its effect) or simultaneously (with its effect) is not a cause; there are ultimately no causes because (ultimate) production is not accepted either conceptually or ultimately."

14 Our translation here partially follows Samten's (57) emendation of the verse. Most versions of the Tengyur read: *ring po yod na thung ngu nyid / rang gi ngo bo las ma yin.* However, based on the non-canonical Zhol version of the text, Samten suggests *thung ngu med na ring po yang / yod min rang bzhin las ma yin.* This agrees with Hahn's Sanskrit edition: *hrasve 'sati punar dīrghaṃ na bhavaty asvabhāvataḥ.* However, all Tibetan canonical versions agree on the line: *rang gi ngo bo las ma yin.* This also accords with Tucci's edition of the Sanskrit: *na bhavati svabhāvataḥ.* Since this reading also yields the clearest meaning, we have followed it. The fully emended Tibetan should thus read: *thung ngu med na ring po yang / rang gi ngo bo las yod min.* Following the canonical versions and Gyaltsab-je (15b-16a), one would get the following translation for the first two lines: "If there is long, there is short; (they) do not exist intrinsically."

15 A translation based on the Sanskrit would read: "Seeing that an effect arises from a cause, one does not accept that (causality) is nonexistent, having provisionally accepted that what is real for the world (just) comes from conceptual fabrication."

16 This translation follows Gyaltsab-je's interpretation of the Tibetan (16a). Following the Sanskrit and Ajitamitra, one arrives at the following translation: "Cessation, since it accords with ultimate reality, is not produced by conceptual fabrication; having obtained it, one will not accept the existence (of the world); therefore, not relying on the two (extremes), one is liberated."

17 An alternative reading, following the Sanskrit, is: "Ask the Sāṃkhyas, Vaiśeṣikas, and Jains, who assert (the real existence) of the person and aggregates, whether they maintain that the world is beyond existence and nonexistence." The Sāṃkhyas, Vaiśeṣikas and Jains are Indian philo-

sophical traditions that espouse the types of realist views which Nāgārjuna seeks to refute.

18 Tib. *khud pa* has senses such as "special gift" or, in older Tibetan, "private" or "personal." Skt. *yautaka*, however, has the specific meaning of "inheritance."

19 This translation follows Ajitamitra and the Sanskrit. Gyaltsab-je (19a) suggests a slightly different reading: "Just as one conceives of a moment as having an end, so too one should conceive of it has having a beginning and middle; thus, since the (momentary) world has the nature of three moments (that are the beginning, middle and end of that moment of the world), the world does not remain for (even) a moment."

20 The term "foundation" renders Tib. *gnas*, Skt. *ālaya*, (the same term that occurs in Skt. *ālayavijñāna*, Tib. *kun gzhi*, "storehouse consciousness" or "foundation consciousness"). We have chosen "foundation" in order to suggest that the worldviews critiqued here include those referred to as "foundationalist" in Euroamerican intellectual traditions.

21 Skt. *tīrthika*, Tib. *mu stegs pa*, is a term used to refer to those who do not accept the teachings of the Buddha. The translation "heretic" which is often given for this term is undesirable as it properly refers to a person who upholds a belief that has been deemed "heretical" by an established institution or church. Since the philosophers to whom the text refers are not persons within the Buddhist tradition who are upholding unacceptable views, the term "heretic" is inappropriate. Apte (*Practical Sanskrit-English Dictionary*) notes that the term *tīrthika* refers to "an adherent or head of any other than one's own creed" (p.776).

22 The six "constituents" (Skt. *dhātu*, Tib. *khams*) are those mentioned in the previous verse: earth, water, fire, wind, space, and consciousness.

23 The four elements (Skt. *mahābhūta*, Tib. *'byung ba bzhi*) are earth, water, fire, and wind.

24 Ajitamitra glosses *gang* as *gang gi phyir*.

25 Another interpretation would read: "If you claim that (only) fire is well known (to depend on fuel), then, according to you, how could (the other) three be independent? It does not make sense for them to be incompatible

with (the fire) that has arisen in dependence upon those three."

26 According to most Indian philosophy, things are comprised of various combinations of the four elements. In each case, the elements are combined in different quantities, such that one or another of the elements is dominant. Here, Nāgārjuna maintains that since none of the elements ultimately exists, none of them can ultimately predominate. Hence, their characteristics must be stated merely in terms of the conventional.

27 This is the technical term in English for the object of an action.

28 Ajitamitra (98) understands "limitless" as an adjective for "awareness." Gyaltsab-je (24b), however, takes "limitless" as the object of "fully sovereign." This type of grammatical issue would be completely clear in Sanskrit (which is not extant for this verse). Hence, it seems best to follow Ajitamitra's interpretation, since his commentary is based on the Sanskrit.

29 This translation is based on the Sanskrit version, which is particularly clear here. Following the Tibetan and Gyaltsab-je's (25a) brief comments, one arrives at the following translation: "Later, one ascertains the suchness (of) that which was previously constructed by ignorance. When the existent is not found, how can there be the nonexistent?"

30 This verse is also translated from the Sanskrit, which presents a more straightforward argument. Following the Tibetan and Gyaltsab-je (25a), one arrives at the following: "Since the things that are forms are merely designations, space is also just a designation. How can there be form without the elements? Therefore, (form) is also just a designation."

31 The Sanskrit differs from the Tibetan in the last two lines. Following the Sanskrit, the verse would read: " Hence, the Victors have said that all things are selfless; they have determined that all six constituents (are selfless), and that those (constituents) are not ultimately (existent)." This reading is supported by Ajitamitra (104).

32 This translation is based upon the Sanskrit, the commentary of Ajitamitra (107), and Samten's emended translation. The last two lines of the canonical Tibetan versions read: *sems can rnam ni bye bar 'gyur / de las dus gsum gnas pa dgongs.* Samten (107), however, proposes the following translation, which is clearly preferable: *dus gsum skyes pa'i sems*

can mtha' / de las bye ba lhag par 'dod.

33 This translation follows the Sanskrit, Ajitamitra (107-8), and the Zhol version of the text, which offers the following reading of the first two lines: *zad pa dus gsum gnas pa ni / 'jig rten 'phel ba'i rgyu ma yin.*

34 Skt. *nīti* refers to the political policies of a king.

35 This translation is based strictly on the interpretation of Gyaltsab-je (31a). However, the number of highly disparate textual variations suggest that there are other plausible readings. On the basis of the manuscripts at our disposal and the commentary of Ajitamitra (125-26), we offer the following alternative: "The truth is not (merely) what is nondeceptive; what is altered by some intention is also not actually true. The truth is what is entirely beneficial to others; anything else is false, in that it is not beneficial." A key variation here is the insertion of an additional negative in the first line, following the editions of both Hahn (52) and Samten (125). Note also Samten's insightful suggestion for interpreting the verse: *sems pas 'du shes bsgyur te smras pa don du bden pa min pa ma zad / slu ba med pa dang ldan pa tsam yang skabs 'dir rgyal pos bsten bya'i bden pa ma yin / 'o na ci zhe na / gzhan la gcig tu phan pa de bden pa dang / mi phan pa ni gcig shos brdzun pa yin no.*

36 This reading follows the Zhol edition and the Sanskrit. The Zhol edition reads: *phan pa myur du byed pa dkon* in place of *phan pa'i rjes su byed pa dkon.* This reading corresponds to the Sanskrit: *ye pathyasyāśukāriṇaḥ.*

37 Gyaltsab-je (31b) interprets *bdag byams pa / mi bzad nga ba'i sman* as *bdag la byams pa / gzhan gyis byin pa'i / mi bzad pa'i dri nga ba'i sman.* From this it is clear that he understands *bdag byams pa* to mean "someone else who loves one." This reading, however, is not supported by either the Sanskrit or Ajitamitra's commentary. The Sanskrit reads, *ātmavān,* which is also clearly the term glossed by Ajitamitra (131); this term means "prudent," "wise," "self-possessed" and so on.

38 Hahn does not include this verse in his edition, calling it spurious (61). He does include it in his notes, however.

39 Ajitamitra (137) glosses *ngan skyugs phag* as a single term. According to the *Bhoṭ-saṃskṛtakoś* (Sarnath, India: Central Institute of Higher

Tibetan Studies, 1995), *ngan skyugs* occurs for *uccāra* and *mīḍha*, both of which mean "filth" or "excrement." Although Hopkins construes it as "vomit," which *skyugs* would mean on its own, this interpretation is not supported by the sources.

40 Both Gyaltsab-je (33a) and Ajitamitra (137) read *gzhi* as *bcer*.

41 Ajitamitra (145) glosses *re ngan* as *smad pa*, "lowly" or "despicable."

42 Skt. *bodhicitta* is the altruistic intention to attain unexcelled awakening for the sake of all sentient beings. The "king of mountains" is Mount Meru, the central mountain of a world-system according to traditional Buddhist cosmology.

43 The Skt. term *caitya* (Tib. *mchod rten*) refers to a type of reliquary in which the physical remains of holy beings or other sacred objects are stored. According to both Gyaltsab-je (36a) and Ajitamitra (148), here a *caitya* is to be construed as a metaphor for a buddha. They both quote a verse that etymologically illustrates this point: *dkar po'i chos rnams bsags phyir dang / sdig pa'i las rnams spang pa'i phyir / sangs rgyas bcom ldan 'das nyid la / mchod rten zhes kyang mngon par brdzod.*

44 To "turn the wheel" is a metaphor employed to indicate two types of exceptional beings: a universal monarch or a perfectly awakened buddha. A universal monarch "turns the wheel" of political power; a perfectly awakened buddha "turns the wheel" of the Dharma.

45 According to Ajitamitra (149) and Gyaltsab-je (36b), these are the two hands, the two feet, the two shoulders and the nape of the neck.

46 The Skt. word *uṣṇīṣa,* literally meaning "turban," refers to a protuberance that appears on the crown of a buddha's head. It is often said that even if one is located above a buddha, one cannot see the top of that buddha's *uṣṇīṣa.*

47 Some versions of the canon read *dbyen dang phra ma med pa*—"that are neither discordant nor divisive."

48 This verse does not appear in the Chinese version, and Gyaltsab-je does not comment upon it. Nevertheless, it appears in all the versions of the canon, and on that basis, Samten has argued for its inclusion. For the specifics of his argument, see his introduction (21). The Zhol version

offers a variant reading: *gtsug tor bsod nams bye ba dag / 'bum phrag brgya ni bsgres pa yis / grangs med brgya chen bcu po dag / sangs rgyas gsung gi sgra dbyangs ni / yan lag drug cu skyed pa'i mchog.* The third line of this five-lined alternative verse is not at all clear. Tentatively, we translate as follows: "The eloquent speech of a buddha, the best of all that gives rise to the sixty aspects (of speech), the ten innumerable and extensive ones (?), arises from the amount of merit that produces the *uṣṇīṣa,* multiplied a million ten millions of times."

49 Ajitamitra (164) interprets "these four" in two possible fashions. According to his first interpretation, they are: truth (*bden pa*), generosity (*gtong ba*), discipline (*dul ba*) and wisdom (*shes rab*). His second interpretation refers to the four things described as infinite in the verse—time (*dus*), beings (*sems can*), the desire for awakening (*byang chub 'dod pa*), and virtue (*dge ba*). Gyaltsab-je (41a) follows the second interpretation.

50 The Zhol, Narthang and Peking editions offer a slightly different reading. Following those editions, the verse would read as follows: "From all kinds of precious substances, please make well drawn and beautifully proportioned images of buddhas seated upon lotuses and adorned with all kinds of gems."

51 See note 21, verse 1.79.

52 Tib. read *zhing bsrtal ba yi nges pa ni.* This is glossed by Ajitamitra (173) as *tshad dam brtan par byas pa.* Apparently, the point here is that the king is asked to grant estates with established borders, probably to avoid land disputes, which were common in India during Nāgārjuna's time.

53 Tib. *'dun khang* = Skt. *maṇḍapa.* One *maṇḍapa* that survives to this day is the famed wooden pavilion in Kathmandu, from which the city derives its name (*kāṣṭhamaṇḍapa* = "wooden pavilion").

54 Ajitamitra (177) seems to suggest that these smaller cisterns are for ants and such.

55 This appears to be a reference to the birth of a being who will become a buddha, for bodhisattvas are said to take seven steps upon being born in the lifetime in which they will become buddhas.

56 The Skt. word *dhāraṇī* refers to a string of syllables that one recites in a

manner similar to a mantra. In some cases, a *dhāraṇī* is thought to have magical properties. In other cases, a *dhāraṇī* simply serves as a mnemonic device that helps one to retain the essential points of a teaching or practice. This second usage reflects the etymology of the word *dhāraṇī*, which is derived from a verb that means "to retain" or "to hold."

57 Tib. *de yi mod* = Skt. *tatkṣaṇa.* Here, this means not "in that moment", but rather "that chance" or "that opportunity."

58 Ajitamitra (183) interprets Tib. *gnad la dbab pa* (= Skt. *marmabheda*) as "publicly speaking of (someone's personal) secret" (*gnad la dbab pa ni gsang ba rab tu sgrogs pa ste*).

59 Ajitamitra (184) glosses *nus pas* as *ci nus kyis.*

60 Tib. *rdze'u tshos.* Samten (188) explains: *rdze'u tshos ni / rtza ma chung ngu du ma'i nang tshos ma rnam grangs du ma btsos pa'i kha zas kyi bye brag go.*

61 Listed by both Ajitamitra (190) and Gyaltsab-je (48b) as molasses, ghee, honey, sesame oil, and salt.

62 The Tibetan word *rol mo* can mean "musical instrument" in general, but it also refers particularly to cymbals. The probable Sanskrit term here is *tūrya*, most commonly meaning "cymbals" in Buddhist literature.

63 Ajitamitra (194) glosses Tib. *don du* as *don gyi sgo nas* = Skt. *arthāt.* The basic meaning of this phrase is "by implication," or "this means that…." Following a more natural Tibetan reading, Gyaltsab-je (49b) interprets it to mean, "for your sake…."

64 With the exception of the Zhol version, the Tibetan translations can be interpreted as follows: "Since it is difficult to know (what a king) will and will not tolerate, most of his subjects praise him, even if he does something that contradicts Dharma, or does something that does not make sense." Our translation is based on the Sanskrit and the Zhol version.

65 Ajitamitra (198) notes that this line can also be interpreted, "Because you are fond of me…."

66 Gyaltsab-je (50a) maintains that the word "steadfast" is vocative, but the available Sanskrit is not in vocative.

67 The phrase "in this context and in others" can be interpreted as meaning

either "in both this life and future lives" or "both for political purposes and for helping the Dharma." See Gyaltsab-je (50a).

68 For Skt. *prāpyārtha* read *prāptārtha.*

69 This translation construes the adjectives "glorious" and "famed" in accord with the grammar of the Sanskrit. Gyaltsab-je (51b) offers a slightly different interpretation: "Establish Dharma-sites and centers of the three jewels; by doing so make yourself glorious and famous in a way not even imagined by weaker kings." A translation based entirely on the Sanskrit would require one further modification based on the term *manoratha*, which is not found in the Tibetan. Such a translation would read: "Establish glorious Dharma-sites and famed centers of the three jewels that have never been experienced by weaker kings, though they wish (that they could build them)."

70 Literally, does not give him "goose-bumps" or cause horripilation.

71 Tib. reads *gsar pa* = *navasya* for Skt. *nṛpasya.*

72 Following the Skt., the last two lines should read: "What you have neither enjoyed nor given will cease (to be yours). Hence, it will bring only suffering—how could it bring happiness?"

73 According to Gyaltsab-je (51a), the description of the ministers as *rjes gnan can* means that they are "shameless." But the Skt. *āyaticchedana* might more plausibly be used to describe the ministers as "those who disregard your future" or "those who destroy your dignity." Following Gyaltsab-je, the verse might also be translated as follows: "When dying you will be unable to give away (your possessions) because you will be rendered impotent by ministers who shamelessly cease to value you and seek the affection of the new king."

74 The translation "truthful, and tolerant" follows Gyaltsab-je's interpretation. The Skt. reads *sarvakṣama*, which might be rendered: "who are skilled in everything," meaning that they are highly competent. An alternative Skt. reading is *satyakṣama*, which means, "who tolerate the truth." This is the reading followed by Ajitamitra (204).

75 Ajitamitra (206) glosses this as *drod zin par spyod pa'am bgo bsha' byas te spyod pa'o.* This interpretation suggests that a military advisor is one who

proceeds with circumspection or delegates authority well.

76 "Disastrous" (Skt. *anartha*) can also be translated as "pointless."

77 Skt. adds "and clothing" (*vasana*).

78 Gyaltsab-je (54a) interprets *rang dbang yod par* as *rang dbang yod par bya bya'i phed du*—"in order to be independent." However, the Tib. verse clearly translates the Skt. *svatantraḥ*, an appositive that means "as one who is independent." In English, this is most easily conveyed with the adverb "independently."

79 Samten (212) notes the variations *rigs pas dpyad na*, "if you analyze rationally...." He remarks, however, that *rigs par spyad na* follows more closely the existing Skt., *evam nyāyād.*

80 Tib. (*'god mi 'gyur*) literally means "will not die." As Samten notes (213), this is apparently meant to convey the meaning of the Sanskrit phrase *mātsyanyāya*, which literally means "in the manner of fish." This maxim or *nyāya* refers to the fact that the larger fish constantly devour the smaller fish—an analogous idiom in English would be "the rule of the jungle."

81 Skt. "a city."

82 Skt. *pradeśa* could be emended to *preṅkhana*, following Tib. *khyog(s)*.

83 This translation follows both Skt. and Tib. Gyaltsab-je (56a) offers a more elaborate interpretation: "When the five faculties such as the eye apprehend their five objects, one does not have (five instances of) pleasure at that (time), because one does not conceptualize (those objects)."

84 "Thus" not found in Skt.

85 Tib. reads "Who sees the mind?" (*gang gyis sems mthong 'gyur zhe na*). However, the Sanskrit, Ajitamitra (221) and Gyaltsab-je (58a) all concur that this should read, "Who sees?" or "Who does this seeing?" Samten notes an alternative translation of this verse found as a quotation in Candrakīrti's *Madhyamakāvatāra.* He quotes as follows: *gang gis mthong bar 'gyur zhe na / tha snyad du ni sems la brjod / sems 'byung med par sems med na / don med phyir na yod mi 'dod.*

86 One could say, "since it is senseless." This follows Ajitamitra's (222) explanation of the last two lines: "If a mental function such as the desire to obtain pleasure were to endure (for more than a moment), then a sec-

ond, later (mental state) could observe it. But if that (former mental function) does not exist (more than a moment), what would be observed? Since it is senseless, we do not accept that two (moments of) mind can occur simultaneously, because (allegedly) simultaneous moments could not stand in the relation of perceived and perceiver since they cease as soon as (they arise)."

87 This follows the Tib. as interpreted by Gyaltsab-je (58b). The Skt. suggests the following translation: "Realizing in this way that the world is ultimately unreal, having no basis, having no cause, one is extinguished like a fire that no (longer) has a cause." Here, in both cases, the word for cause is *upādāna*, which can be translated as "appropriation" in the context of rebirth, where it refers to the process of obtaining new aggregates.

88 Skt. *sambhāra*, Tib. *tshog*. The two "collections" that a bodhisattva needs in order to become a buddha are the collection of merit (*puṇyasambhāra*) and the collection of wisdom (*jñānasambhāra*).

89 In accord with the Skt. (*svārthanirapekṣatvāt*) and Gyaltsab-je (59b), we follow the Zhol edition's reading of *mi lta phyir* for *mi lta zhing*.

90 Literally, "is burned," but Skt. *dahyate* can mean "is tormented."

91 Skt., *dhīra* can also mean "steadfast," "resolute" and so on.

92 This is clearly the meaning of this line in Skt., but as Gyaltsab-je notes (60b), the Tib. can be interpreted to mean "and it speaks of stainless wisdom."

93 Skt., *puṇya*, "merit."

94 Skt., *ātmakāmaiḥ* "those who love themselves...."

95 Tib. could be interpreted as singular, but Skt. *buddhair* is definitely plural.

96 Tib. "bases" but Skt., *adhiṣṭhāna*.

97 Tib. *ji tsam bzod* means "to the degree that they could tolerate," but Skt. *yathākṣamam* means "according to (their) abilities)." Although in some contexts *kṣama* does mean "tolerance," here it has the meaning of "ability."

98 Skt adds: "and truth...."

99 This translation is based on the Skt., which is accurately reflected by the Tib. However, Gyaltsab-je (64b-65a) interprets the Tib. differently: "Thereupon, as a monk you should first become serious about the train-

ing (in higher morality). Then focus on the *Pratimokṣa* along with the *Vinaya*, also on becoming learned and determining the meaning (of what you study)." The *Pratimokṣa* (or *Prātimokṣa*) is a condensed form of the monastic code. The *Vinaya* refers to the complete collection of all the basic texts on monasticism.

100 The translation of the first two lines follows Gyaltsab-je (65a). However, his interpretation is based on an anomaly in the Tibetan translation concerning *shes bya ba*, which is an accurate translation of the Skt. *-saṃjñita*, "named" or "so called." In order to keep the proper number of syllables in the first line, the original translators broke shes bya ba into two separate lines. Hence, the first two lines read: *de nas nyes pa phran tshegs shes / bya ba'i gzhi rnams spang bar bya.* Due to this line break, the *shes* at the end of the first line appears to be unrelated to the *bya ba* at the beginning of the second line. As a result, Gyaltsab-je treated them as separate words: *shes*, meaning "aware" or "knowing," and *bya ba*, "should be done" or "is to be done," etc. In fact, the *shes* and *bya ba* should be construed together, since together they translate the single Skt. term *-saṃjñita.* In addition, the syntax of the Tibetan translation as it stands is misleading about the word *gzhi*, which Gyaltsab-je interprets as "basis," in the sense of a basic cause. The Tibetan syntax suggests that the "basis" is being called "small" (*phran tshegs*), but this is not supported by the Skt., which reads: *tato doṣāḥ prahātavyāḥ kṣudravastukasaṃjñitāḥ.* It is clear here that "small" (*kṣudra*) and "basis" (*vastuka*) should be read together. This makes it clear that the term "basis" (*vastu*) here actually refers to a kind of omnibus or collection of various topics. One example of such a text is the *Vinayavastu* (Tib., *dul ba'i gleng gzhi*). The text referred to in this verse is the *Kṣudravastuka*, a collection of "small" or "assorted" topics. It is one of the earliest texts to give a systematic listing of primary and secondary negative mental states. Vasubandu mentions it in his *Abhidharmakośabhāṣya* (for example, on 5.47; see Derge edition, f. 250a). With this in mind, the Sanskrit *Kṣudravastukasaṃjñitāḥ* cannot refer to faults that are "called *kṣudravastuka*." Instead, the verse refers to faults that are "named (or cited) in the *Kṣudravastuka*." Hence, it is perhaps

best to emend the Tib. of the first two lines as follows: *de nas phran tshegs kyi gzhi las / bshad pa'i nyes pa spang bar bya.* This yields the following translation, which seems to make the most sense: "Then you should eliminate those faults which are cited in the *Kṣudravastuka.*"

101 For Skt. "fury" (*saṃrambha*) Tib. reads "flawed effort" (*nyes rtsom*). For Skt. "mental disturbance" (*vibhrama*) Tib. reads "polluted (state of mind)" (*bslad pa*).

102 Or, to follow the Skt. more closely, "particularly presumptuous even for what is presumptuous."

103 Skt. replaces "empty" with "aggregates."

104 Ajitamitra (241) remarks, "*dgos pa med pa ni mi nus pa'o.*"

105 Skt. *prakopita* should perhaps read *praskhalita*, attested by *Bhoṭ-saṃskṛtakoś* (Central Institute of Higher Tibetan Studies, Sarnath, p. 458).

106 Tib. *slong ba* means just "agitated," but Skt. *viklavībhāva* means "being overwhelmed."

107 These last two lines are based on the Tib. The following translation from the Skt. may make more sense as an explanation of "stupefaction": "or else it is a lazy person's attachment to sleep when he is deprived of what he needs to support himself."

108 The Skt. and Tib. agree on this verse, but the Tib. syntax led Gyaltsab-je (66b) to take a different interpretation.

109 For both instances of Skt. "greed" (*lobha*) in this verse, Tib. reads "attachment" (*chags pa*).

110 Skt., *icchepsutā.* Tib., *tob 'dod* means, "desire for gain."

111 This is based on Tib. According to the Skt., one would translate, "...one does not take it seriously that the statements which have been spoken are the holy Dharma." Following Gyaltsab-je (67a), one would translate, "...one does not take seriously the statements made by one who is in accord with Dharma."

112 Tib. *yul* can mean either "object" or "country"; however, Skt. *jānapada* can mean only "country" or "district." The sense of "overstate" comes from Skt. *atyartha*, but Tib. has only *de don du*, "for its sake" (probably from Skt. *tadartham*). Without access to the Skt., Gyaltsab-je (67a) was

obliged to choose between the meanings of Tib. *yul* as "country" and "object." He decided to interpret it as "object." On his interpretation, the first two lines mean, "Likewise, to crave an object is to state / its good qualities for the sake of [obtaining] it."

113 We follow Samten's preference for the Zhol reading of "longing" (*phrad 'dod*, Skt., *samutkaṇṭhā*). See Samten's note (347, n.1) on Gyaltsab-je, whose interpretation we do not follow here.

114 For Skt. "it comes from being physically listless" (*gātrāvasādottham*); Tib. reads, "it means being physically listless." We feel the Skt. reading makes more sense than the Tib., in that the point here is that this particular type of laziness arises from being physically inactive or exhausted. As Samten points out (247, n.5), one may account for the difference between the Tib. and Skt. by noting that in a number of Indian scripts it is quite easy to confuse *-ottham* with *-ārtham*.

115 Skt. reads "desire for food," which is confirmed by the Chinese translation. However, Ajitamitra confirms the reading we have translated. In view of the definition given here, one must wonder whether *bhaktasaṃmūḍha*, "stupefied by (eating too much) food," might be a possible reading.

116 For "physical stupor" (*kāyasya mūrcchana*) Tib. reads "physical discomfort" (*lus mi bde ba*), which was probably chosen as a gloss for *murcchana*.

117 Skt. "sincc" (*hi*) is abscnt in Tib.

118 As Samten (253) notes, this verse may be a later addition to the text. In the currently available Tib. editions, only two lincs of thc vcrsc appcar, but the remainder is preserved in the Skt. Samten has translated the remaining two lines into Tibetan, and we have decided to include all four lines of the verse.

119 This interpretation follows Ajitamitra (255), who remarks: "The source of the belief that the transitory aggregates (are the self) refers to its cause—it is ignorance, since that is what (that belief) arises from."

120 The translation of the last two lines follows Ajitamitra (256). Gyaltsab-je (70b) interprets, "...and refutes the bases of the negative mental states and beliefs of all the Tīrthikas."

121 This is translated according to Gyaltsab-je (71a). But Ajitamitra (257)

notes, "this means that s/he is one who possesses excellent emanations." Ajitamitra's comment agrees with the Skt., *devarājaḥ sunirmitaḥ*, which means, "a celestial ruler with excellent emanations."

122 Ajitamitra (258) understands "powerful" (Skt. *vaśavartin*, Tib., *dbang sgyur*) to mean "having control over negative mental states or (meditative) cessation." However, Gyaltsab-je (71a) may understand this term to refer to the heaven in which dwell the celestials who control others' emanations.

123 Ajitamitra (264) comments: "'Supreme person' means a buddha because a buddha is superior to all beings. Or else it means any other kind of supreme person not included in the (category of buddhahood)."

124 Gyaltsab-je (73b) interprets 'intelligence' as a metaphor for the higher training in wisdom and 'legs' as a metaphor for morality. Ajitamitra (264-5) offers three interpretations: "'Intelligence' means the proper view; 'legs' refers to the remaining aspects (of the path). Or 'intelligence' means the divine eye and divine ear; and 'legs' refers to the remaining (special powers). Or 'intelligence' means the special intention (to achieve awakening for all beings); and 'legs' refers to the rest (of the bodhisattva's attributes)."

125 Tib. *nyon mongs* translates Skt. *kleśa*, which means either "negative mental states" or "pain," "hardship," and so on. According to Gyaltsab-je's interpretation (73b), this phrase refers to the ability to "remain in the equanimity that is devoid of negative mental states."

126 This follows Gyaltsab-je's (266) interpretation. Ajitamitra (266) interprets, "and as a loving one, superior to all beings...."

127 For Tib. "thinking" (*dran pa*, literally, "remembering"), Skt. reads "touching" (*sparśana*).

128 Some versions and Ajitamitra (267) read "undisturbed" (*'khrug med*); other versions and Gyaltsab-je read "not confused" (*khrul med*). Skt. reads "disturbed," which is probably a scribal error. The translation "at ease" renders Skt. *svastha*, interpreted by Ajitamitra (267) as "not distracted." *Svastha* also means "comfortable," "healthy," "happy," "self-controlled" and so on. Tib. *rnal ma* means "natural," which is an indirect meaning of *svastha*.

129 Skt. "single" (*eka*) not recorded in Tib.

130 The placement of *iti* at the beginning of this verse indicates that Nāgārjuna has finished the main topic of this text.

131 For Skt. "yourself" (*ātman*), Tib. reads "(your own) body" (*sku*). However, in view of the next verse, "yourself" seems to make more sense than "body." This is supported by Ajitamitra's interpretation (270-271).

132 The translation of this verse follows the Skt. (reading either *svakārtham* or *svakīyam* for ms. *svakāyam*). The third line could also be rendered, "...that says what is helpful for those who need correction...." Following the Tib. and Gyaltsab-je (75b), we translate: "One who has doubts that (relying on a teacher who is) pure, loving, and intelligent, and who speaks with intellectual confidence about what is beneficial, is ruining his own aims." Gyaltsab-je apparently had *spob pas* (Skt, *pratibhāna*, "intellectual confidence") for mss. *phebs pas*.

133 This verse is absent in the Zhol edition, and it is not mentioned by either Ajitamitra or Gyaltsab-je. We have followed the Tib. of the last line. The Skt., which may be corrupt, reads *nṛpate niryātyātmānam āśvasa*. "Through renunciation, king, grant yourself relief (from suffering)."

134 "skilled in public policy" renders Skt. *nītimant*.

135 Skt. *sudāntānuśaya*. This phrase might also mean, "with negative proclivities well subdued." A "negative proclivity" (Skt. *anuśaya*, Tib. *bag la nyal ba*) refers to the latent potentials of negative mental states. The Tib. syntax of the translation is somewhat confusing, but Gyaltsab-je construes this phrase as meaning, "without enmity" (*khon du 'dzin pa med pa*).

136 See Samten (274, n.4) on misprint of *des pa* as *nges pa*.

137 Here again, *des pa* is often misprinted as *nges pa*. See Samten (274, n.5).

138 For Tib. "to contemplate" (*bsam pa*), Skt. reads "to listen to" (*śrotum*).

139 Gyaltsab-je (76b) construes "highest" (*mchog*) with "gurus," but in the Skt. it clearly modifies "respect."

140 The final verse of the *Precious Garland* has been composed in *śārdūlavikrīḍita* meter which in Sanskrit has nineteen syllables per metrical "foot."

141 This line may also be translated, "There is nothing other than one truth."

Śākyamuni Buddha

Brief Remarks on the Śākyamuni Empowerment

Among the many forms of meditation within Tibetan Buddhism, some of the most popular and efficacious involve the use of visualizations. In many cases, meditators visualize a particular figure that personifies some aspect of the Buddhist path. These figures are tremendously diverse, for they embody a great variety of practices designed to address the particular needs and propensities of practitioners as they progress in their spiritual development.

Some of the most widely practiced forms of visualization focus on the figure of the historical Buddha, Śākyamuni. As the founder of Buddhism as we know it, Śākyamuni embodies the basic qualities that all Buddhists seek to obtain. At the same time, the figure of Śākyamuni can be said to represent the fundamental teachings of Buddhism, often summarized in this famous verse:

Do not engage in any negativity;
develop full and perfect virtue;
completely transform your mind—
this is the Buddha's teaching.

To introduce participants to a practice focusing on Śākyamuni Buddha, His Holiness the Dalai Lama will confer an empowerment—ritual that prepares or "blesses" one's mind for the practice. Through the visualizations taught during the empowerment, participants will also learn the basic content and meaning of this form of meditation. As with most such practices, this meditation on Śākyamuni Buddha also involves a *mantra*, a series of syllables that one recites to focus one's mind on the practice. Reflecting the Indian origins of these practices, *mantras* are based upon Sanskrit, the ancient language of India. For the practice of Śākyamuni Buddha, the most common mantra is based upon the Sanskrit word *muni*, meaning "the sage." The mantra is:

OṂ MUNI MUNI MAHĀ MUNAYE SVĀHĀ

For those who actually wish to practice this form of meditation, this empowerment can serve to initiate them into the practice. But according to the Tibetan tradition, even those who do not intend to engage in this practice may still participate in the empowerment as a form of blessing and spiritual encouragement.

About His Holiness
the Fourteenth Dalai Lama of Tibet

Venerable Tenzin Gyatso, who describes himself as a "simple Buddhist monk," is widely recognized to be both the spiritual and the temporal leader of the Tibetan people. Known more popularly in the West as the Dalai Lama, and among Tibetans as Yeshe Norbu ("Wish-fulfilling Jewel"), Venerable Tenzin Gyatso attained worldwide recognition in 1989 when he was awarded the Nobel Peace Prize for his dedication to a non-violent struggle for the liberation of Tibet. Speaking and writing eloquently on the need for a commitment to compassion and a sense of universal responsibility, the fourteenth Dalai Lama travels extensively and frequently visits the United States.

Born in 1935 to a poor family in northeastern Tibet, the present Dalai Lama was recognized at age three to be the most recent in a line of thirteen previous Dalai Lamas, each of whom has been considered to be an incarnation of Avalokiteśvara, the bodhisattva of compassion. At age five, Tenzin Gyatso was enthroned as the new Dalai Lama in Lhasa, the capital of Tibet, and at the same time received his first monastic vows. In 1950, when he was only fifteen, Tenzin Gyatso assumed full leadership of his country in the face of a Chinese invasion of its eastern border. Over the next nine years, the Dalai Lama attempted to negotiate with Chinese Communist leaders such as Mao Tse-Tung to save his country, but to no avail. In 1959, Chinese troops violently suppressed an uprising of the Tibetan people in Lhasa, and the Dalai Lama was forced to flee into exile in India. The Indian government granted him and his people refuge, and the Dalai Lama, along with the Tibetan Government-in-Exile, has resided in Dharamsala, India ever since.

As a religious leader, the Dalai Lama was educated primarily within the Geluk-pa school of Tibetan Buddhism, receiving the highest rank within that school's monastic curriculum, the Geshe Lharampa degree, in 1959. In addition to his Gelukpa education, the Dalai Lama has also received extensive teachings from the most revered lamas of the Kagyu, Sakya, and Nyingma traditions, and in his own philosophical writings he proposes ways to integrate the practices and teachings of these various schools. Similarly, a firm conviction that humanity shares a single nature of basic goodness has led the Dalai Lama to engage in interreligious dialogue with leading practitioners from traditions such as Christianity, Judaism, and Hinduism. Finally, his long-standing interest in science and technology has led him to pursue discussions with scientists from around the world on topics ranging from cognitive neurology to physics.

Applying Buddhist principles to the political crises that have plagued his country since 1950, the fourteenth Dalai Lama proposed his Five Point Peace Plan in an address to the U.S. Congress in 1987. According to the plan, Tibet would become a demilitarized zone of peace and the Tibetan people would be permitted to practice their religion freely; the plan also proposed negotiations between the Chinese government and the Tibetan government-in-exile. The plan was quickly denounced in Beijing, leading to demonstrations in Lhasa and a crackdown by Chinese police. But despite the harshness of the Chinese rule in Tibet, the Dalai Lama continues to insist on the need for a non-violent solution; indeed, he constantly proclaims that the proper response toward the Chinese government is not one of anger or hated but rather one of heartfelt compassion and love.

Thubten Dhargye Ling and Venerable Geshe Gyeltsen

The Venerable Geshe Tsultim Gyeltsen founded Thubten Dhargye Ling, a center for the study of Buddhism and Tibetan culture located in Los Angeles, California, in 1978. Since then, the center has hosted numerous events, inviting many great Tibetan Buddhist teachers of the highest learning and realization. Foremost among all these is His Holiness the Dalai Lama. The present event marks the fourth time that Thubten Dhargye Ling has had the honor of sponsoring teachings by His Holiness the Dalai Lama in Los Angeles.

In 1978, His Holiness gave teachings on the *Eight Verses on Thought Training* at Thubten Dhargye Ling. In 1984, he returned to Los Angeles at Geshe Gyeltsen's invitation to teach on the *Three Principle Aspects of the Path* and to confer an Avalokiteśvara initiation. His Holiness then returned in July, 1989, to confer the Kālacakra initiation. Thubten Dhargye Ling is extremely pleased and honored to be able to host this fourth teaching by His Holiness in June, 1997, consisting of a teaching on Nāgārjuna's *Precious Garland* and a Śākyamuni initiation.

Thubten Dhargye Ling continually sponsors many other events of interest for students of Buddhism and Tibetan culture. In 1997, the center co-sponosred a seven week course at UCLA Extension. Entitled "Buddhism and the Modern World," the course featured teachers from seven of the Buddhist traditions represented in Los Angeles and several lectures from teachers with backgrounds in the sciences.

Geshe Tsultim Gyeltsen was born in eastern Tibet in 1923. At age seven, he entered the local monastery, Chamdo Geden Champa

Ling. At sixteen, he traveled to central Tibet to continue his studies at Ganden Monastic University in Lhasa, where he eventually earned the highest degree in the Gelukpa tradition, the Geshe Lharampa degree.

Geshe Gyeltsen was still at Ganden as a teacher of younger monks when the Communist Chinese occupation of Tibet began. In March 1959, Geshe-la joined His Holiness the Dalai Lama and thousands of other Tibetans and walked across the Himalayas to freedom in India. In India, the Tibetan people established a government in exile. Schools and monasteries were rebuilt and new institutions were founded. The new government in exile requested Geshe Gyeltsen to travel abroad to teach at a Tibetan children's school in England. In the mid nineteen-seventies, Geshe Gyeltsen moved to southern California, where he presently resides.

Those interested in further information about Geshe Gyeltsen or Thubten Dhargye Ling may contact the center at:

Thubten Dhargye Ling Monastery, Library, and Bookstore
3500 East 4th Street
Long Beach, CA 90803
(562) 621-9856

Acknowledgments and Sponsors

The success of His Holiness the Dalai Lama's visit to Los Angeles for these teachings is the result of the hard work, dedication and cooperation of many people—too many to name individually. To each of them the students of Thubten Dhargye Ling send heartfelt thanks. In particular, we thank our compassionate guru, His Holiness the 14th Dalai Lama of Tibet. May your good health continue and your precious life be long. May every thought in your mind quickly become a reality, especially your wishes for your people and your country.

We also thank our beloved teacher and spiritual friend, Venerable Geshe Tsultim Gyeltsen, who invited His Holiness to return to Los Angeles to teach and allowed us the opportunity to organize this event.

May you, too, have a long and healthy life. May the immeasurable merit of your Dharma actions increase wihout end to bring benefit to all.

In addition, the following people have helped in many ways to make these teachings a reality: Tenzin Geyche Tethong and the staff at His Holiness's office; Dawa Tsering, Representative of His Holiness the Dalai Lama and the staff at the Office of Tibet; Rinchen Dharlo and the Tibet Fund; Venerable Tenzin Dakpa of Namgyal Monastery; Venerable Tenzin Tokme of Namgyal Monastery; Ganden Shartse Monastery; Los Angeles Friends of Tibet; Tibet Association of Southern California; Vajrapani Institute; Wisdom Publications; The Los Angeles area Tibetan Buddhist Centers; Southern California Buddhist Sangha Council; Cerrell Associates; Ken Chang; DC Printing; Ricardo

DeAratanha; Carlos Gonzalez; Richard Keyes Design;Jacob Maarse Florist; Chris Michaels Catering; Francesca Murphy.

Our generous sponsors (as of April 14, 1997) include: John W. Allen; Bernard Altshuler; Arthur Azdair; R. Lawrence Bacon and Sharon Brown Bacon; Don Brown; Celia T. Chung; Jean Copeland; Gail Cottman/National Satellite Productions; Jeane Day; Elinor (Dufy) Defibaugh; John Dugger/Banner Arts; Robert Duvall; Laurence Eggers; Maria Florio; Oma Darlene Ford; Paula Fouce; the Gere Foundation; Steven Ginsberg and Katharine Payne; Dan and Tara Goleman; Louise Hagihara; Frank Hanulec; Doren and Mary Harper; Goldie Hawn; Heron Foundation; Barry and Connie Hershey; Marika Hirai; Ray Hirata; Rena Kuhn/Monasteries in Tibet Fund; Suzanne La Pierre; Maarlea Monon Li; Mami Y. Mc Gee; Carol Moss; Victoria Mudd; Hy and Lee Pham; Margie Potegian; Jennie R. Quan; Toby Rhodes; Diana V. Rogers; Alex Rose; Martin and Carol Rubin; Leonard Schwartzman, M.D.; Steven Seagal; Fred Segal; Will Spiegelman and Anne Bergman; Kirk Stambler and Victoria Tennant; Sharon Stone; Jan Greer Sullivan; Tom Thorning; Travelers Foundation; Julia M. Wong; Dr. M. Lonnie Wu; Peggy Wu; Paul P. Zanowiak, D.D.S. (Dr. Z).

May benefactors of the Dharma live long
and continue to manifest to support the sublime teachings of the all-good Buddha Shakyamuni.
May all beings be happy.

About Wisdom Publications

Wisdom Publications, a not-for-profit publisher, is dedicated to making available authentic Buddhist works for the benefit of all. We publish translations of the sutras and tantras, commentaries and teachings of past and contemporary Buddhist masters, and original works by the world's leading Buddhist scholars. We publish our titles with the appreciation of Buddhism as a living philosophy and with the special commitment to preserve and transmit important works from all the major Buddhist traditions.

If you would like more information or a copy of our mail order catalog, please write or call us at:

Wisdom Publications
361 Newbury Street
Boston, Massachusetts, 02115 USA
Telephone: (617) 536-3358
Fax: (617) 536-1897
E-mail: info@wisdompubs.org
Web Site: http://www.wisdompubs.org

The Wisdom Trust

As a not-for-profit publisher, Wisdom Publications is dedicated to the publication of fine Dharma books for the benefit of all sentient beings and dependent upon the kindness and generosity of sponsors in order to do so. If you would like to make a donation to Wisdom please contact our Boston office.

Thank you

Wisdom Publications is a non-profit, charitable 501(c)3 organization and a part of the Foundation for the Preservation of the Mahayana Tradition (FPMT).